FIRST FUN
THESAURUS

Cindy Leaney

Miles Kelly
PUBLISHING

How to use your thesaurus

Your thesaurus is a book about words. It will help you to use new or different words when you are writing or talking. It does this by giving you a choice of words that have similar, but not the same, meanings. Every page has a new keyword with a choice of related words called branchwords, or synonyms. You can decide which word is the right one. Each branchword is explained and placed in an example sentence to show how you can use it. You will also find word opposites, or antonyms. There are cartoons, games and fact panels throughout your book.

Keyword and branchwords

There is a new keyword on every page. Each keyword is in large type, and is followed by a wavy line of branchwords. Every word is in alphabetical order.

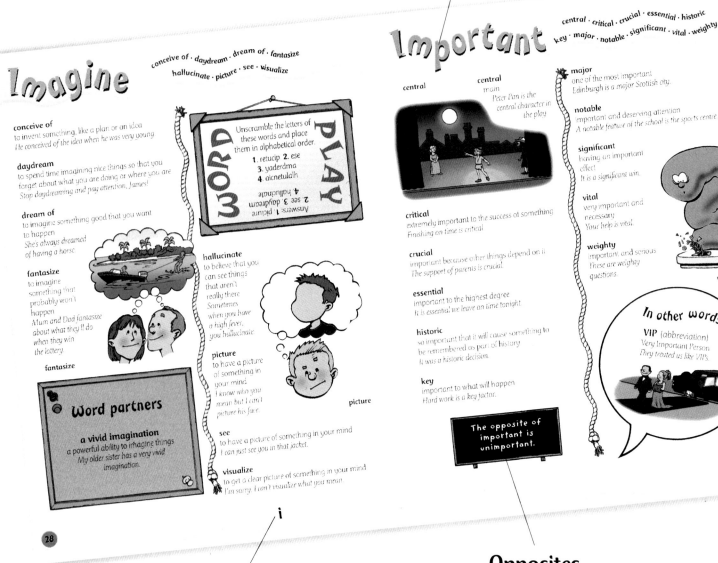

Imagine

conceive of · daydream · dream of · fantasize
hallucinate · picture · see · visualize

conceive of
to invent something, like a plan or an idea
He conceived of the idea when he was very young

daydream
to spend time imagining nice things so that you forget about what you are doing or where you are
Stop daydreaming and pay attention, James!

dream of
to imagine something good that you want to happen
She's always dreamed of having a horse.

fantasize
to imagine something that probably won't happen
Mum and Dad fantasize about what they'll do when they win the lottery.

fantasize

WORD PLAY
Unscramble the letters of these words and place them in alphabetical order.
1. retucip 2. ese
3. yaderdma
4. aicnetulalh

Answers: 1. picture 2. see 3. daydream 4. hallucinate

hallucinate
to believe that you can see things that aren't really there
Sometimes when you have a high fever, you hallucinate.

picture
to have a picture of something in your mind
I know who you mean but I can't picture his face.

picture

see
to have a picture of something in your mind
I can just see you in that jacket.

visualize
to get a clear picture of something in your mind
I'm sorry, I can't visualize what you mean.

Word partners
a vivid imagination
a powerful ability to imagine things
My older sister has a very vivid imagination.

28

i

Important

central · critical · crucial · essential · historic
key · major · notable · significant · vital · weighty

central

central
main
Peter Pan is the central character in the play

critical
extremely important to the success of something
Finishing on time is critical

crucial
important because other things depend on it
The support of parents is crucial.

essential
important to the highest degree
It is essential we leave on time tonight.

historic
so important that it will cause something to be remembered as part of history
It was a historic decision.

key
important to what will happen
Hard work is a key factor.

major
one of the most important
Edinburgh is a major Scottish city.

notable
important and deserving attention
A notable feature of the school is the sports centre

significant
having an important effect
It is a significant win.

vital
very important and necessary
Your help is vital.

weighty
important and serious
These are weighty questions.

weighty

In other words
VIP (abbreviation)
Very Important Person
They treated us like VIPs.

The opposite of important is unimportant.

Alphabetical order

The words in this book are in alphabetical order. The coloured band along the bottom of every page will tell you which letter of the alphabet you are looking at. A list of all the words in your thesaurus can be found in the index at the back of the book.

Opposites

There are small blackboard panels throughout your book. These give the opposites of the keywords.

FIRST FUN
THESAURUS

First published in 2002
By Miles Kelly Publishing Ltd
Bardfield Centre
Great Bardfield
Essex CM7 4SL

2 4 6 8 10 9 7 5 3 1

British Library Cataloguing-in-Publication Data
A catalogue record for this book is available from the British Library

ISBN 1-84236-117-1

Printed in Hong Kong

Author
Cindy Leaney

Project Management
Belinda Gallagher

Editorial Assistant
Nicola Jessop

Copy Editor
Anne Kay

Proofreader
Lynn Bresler

Art Director
Clare Sleven

Designer
Julie Francis

Artist
Mike Foster/Maltings Partnership

www.mileskelly.net
info@mileskelly.net

Did you know?

These give interesting information about words, where they came from and how old they are.

Entries

Each branchword is explained and placed in an example sentence to show you how it could be used.

Word play

Look for the word play picture frames to play games, solve puzzles and have fun with words.

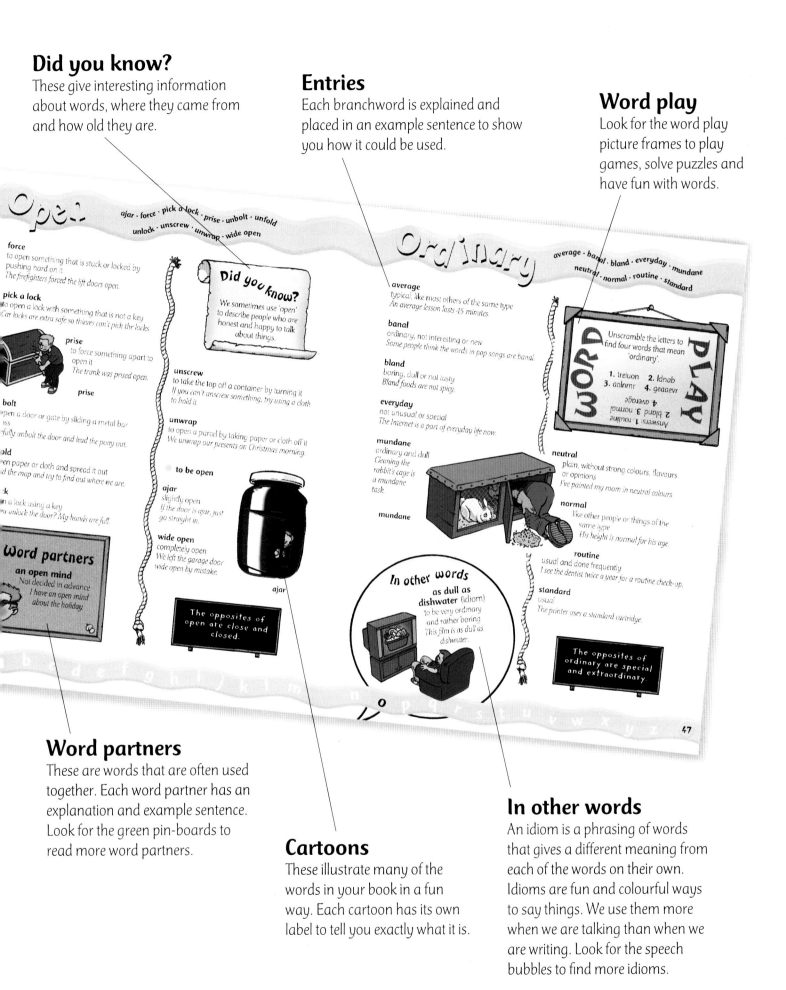

Open
ajar · force · pick a lock · prise · unbolt · unfold
unlock · unscrew · unwrap · wide open

force
to open something that is stuck or locked by pushing hard on it
The firefighters forced the lift doors open.

pick a lock
to open a lock with something that is not a key
Car locks are extra safe so thieves can't pick the locks.

prise
to force something apart to open it
The trunk was prised open.

prise

bolt
open a door or gate by sliding a metal bar
[...]
[...] unbolt the door and lead the pony out.

old
[op]en paper or cloth and spread it out
[...] the map and try to find out where we are.

[lo]ck
[...] a lock using a key
[...]u unlock the door? My hands are full.

Did you know?
We sometimes use 'open' to describe people who are honest and happy to talk about things.

unscrew
to take the top off a container by turning it
If you can't unscrew something, try using a cloth to hold it.

unwrap
to open a parcel by taking paper or cloth off it
We unwrap our presents on Christmas morning.

to be open

ajar
slightly open
If the door is ajar, just go straight in.

wide open
completely open
We left the garage door wide open by mistake.

ajar

Word partners

an open mind
Not decided in advance
I have an open mind about the holiday.

The opposites of open are close and closed.

Ordinary
average · banal · bland · everyday · mundane
neutral · normal · routine · standard

average
typical, like most others of the same type
An average lesson lasts 45 minutes.

banal
ordinary, not interesting or new
Some people think the words in pop songs are banal.

bland
boring, dull or not tasty
Bland foods are not spicy.

everyday
not unusual or special
The Internet is a part of everyday life now.

mundane
ordinary and dull
Cleaning the rabbit's cage is a mundane task.

mundane

WORD PLAY
Unscramble the letters to find four words that mean 'ordinary'.
1. treiuon
2. ldnab
3. aolnmr
4. geaaevr
Answers: 1. routine 2. bland 3. normal 4. average

neutral
plain, without strong colours, flavours or opinions
I've painted my room in neutral colours.

normal
like other people or things of the same type
His height is normal for his age.

routine
usual and done frequently
I see the dentist twice a year for a routine check-up.

standard
usual
The printer uses a standard cartridge.

The opposites of ordinary are special and extraordinary.

In other words
as dull as dishwater (idiom)
to be very ordinary and rather boring
This film is as dull as dishwater.

47

Word partners

These are words that are often used together. Each word partner has an explanation and example sentence. Look for the green pin-boards to read more word partners.

Cartoons

These illustrate many of the words in your book in a fun way. Each cartoon has its own label to tell you exactly what it is.

In other words

An idiom is a phrasing of words that gives a different meaning from each of the words on their own. Idioms are fun and colourful ways to say things. We use them more when we are talking than when we are writing. Look for the speech bubbles to find more idioms.

Angry

annoyed · cross · furious · indignant · irate · irritated
livid · mad · resentful · seething

● **feeling a little angry**

annoyed
feeling slightly angry or impatient
Arran will be annoyed if we forget her birthday.

cross
feeling a little angry
Our teacher gets cross when we are naughty.

cross

irritated
feeling annoyed about something that keeps happening
I'm really irritated – this game keeps crashing.

● **feeling angry or very angry**

furious
extremely angry
There was a furious row going on.

irate
to feel angry because something has upset you
The Internet company received a lot of irate emails from angry customers.

WORD PLAY

Put these words in the right order, from very, very angry down to just a little bit angry:

a. annoyed **b.** furious **c.** mad

Answers: **b c a**

In other words

to have steam coming out of your ears (idiom)
to be really angry about something
Wow! You could almost see the steam coming out of his ears!

livid
to feel so angry that you can't think
Angry? She was livid!

mad
angry
This DVD player makes me so mad!

seething
to be very angry without saying anything
He was so tense, you could tell he was seething.

● **feeling upset because something is wrong or not fair**

indignant
feeling angry because something is wrong, unfair or insulting
Many parents wrote indignant letters when the playgroup closed.

resentful
feeling angry about something that is unfair and that you cannot change
Some of us resent the new rules, but we all have to follow them.

a

Argue

bicker · clash · dispute · feud · fight · quarrel · row
squabble · spat · tiff

● to argue

bicker
an argument that isn't too serious
They bickered about who should have won the game.

clash
to fight or argue in public
The rioters clashed with police.

fight / row
to argue noisily
Why are you always fighting with your brother?

quarrel
to argue with a friend or someone in your family
They quarrelled over whose turn it was to play.

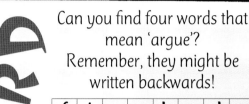

WORD PLAY

Can you find four words that mean 'argue'?
Remember, they might be written backwards!

f	i	g	e	b	c	d	e
i	v	d	d	r	e	r	u
g	s	t	u	s	p	a	t
h	t	o	e	u	i	o	o
t	i	f	f	o	o	t	p
s	f	e	e	d	d	s	u

Answers: **fight feud tiff spat**

squabble
to argue about something that is not important
Stop squabbling over those sweets!

squabble

● an argument

dispute
an official fight between groups or countries
The dispute was about land.

feud
a long fight between two groups or families
No one can remember why the family feud started.

spat / tiff
a small argument
It was just a tiff — it will soon blow over.

In other words
to fight like cat and dog (idiom)
to argue all the time
My sister and brother fight like cat and dog.

7

 # Ask

● **to ask**

consult
to ask for advice or information from an expert
Consult your doctor first.

enquire
to ask for information
Tourists can enquire at the information centre.

interrogate
to ask someone a lot of questions about a crime
The police interrogated the suspect for hours.

interview
to ask someone questions for a newspaper or TV programme, or to find out if they are right for a job
The manager interviewed everyone who applied for the job.

plead
to ask someone for something that you really want
The children pleaded with their mother for some more chocolate.

poll
a study that asks a lot of people about their opinion of something
The poll shows 75% of people agree with the laws.

pump
to ask someone a lot of questions to get as much information as possible
We pumped them for all the information about the new campsite.

> **The opposite of ask is answer.**

plead

query
to ask because you have not understood something or do not think it is right
They queried the bill.

question
to ask someone a lot of questions
The headmaster questioned each pupil about who had broken the window.

quiz
to ask someone a lot of questions about something, usually in an annoying way
They quizzed us about the new teacher.

survey
to ask a lot of people a set of questions
We surveyed the school and found that most children have a mobile phone.

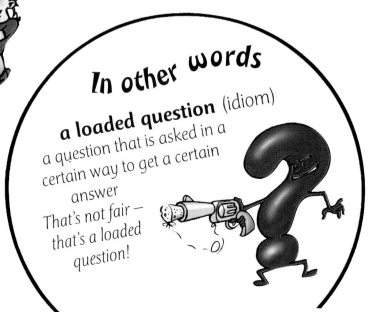

In other words

a loaded question (idiom)
a question that is asked in a certain way to get a certain answer
That's not fair – that's a loaded question!

a b

In other words

have a bad hair day (idiom)
a funny way to say that your hair is in a mess and everything is going wrong.
I'm having a really bad hair day!

● **something that is bad**

appalling
something that is bad in a shocking way
The prisoners' quarters were appalling.

dreadful
something that is very unpleasant or low quality
It's a dreadful film – don't go to see it.

ghastly
very unpleasant or shocking
That's a violent, ghastly game!

terrible
very unpleasant or frightening
It was a terrible storm.

● **bad at doing something**

inept
not skilled (formal)
The inept goalkeeper let in six goals.

hopeless/useless
not good at something (informal)
I'm useless at maths, I can't even do simple sums.

Did you know?

The scientist Albert Einstein was useless at maths when he was young.

● **something that is not good quality**

inferior
not as good as something or someone else
These trainers are cheaper but they're inferior, too.

● **badly behaved**

naughty
badly behaved, usually about a child
It's very naughty to hit someone.

The opposite of bad is good.

Call

cry · name · phone · ring · scream · shout · shriek · summon · yell

● **to say something in a loud voice**

cry
to speak in a loud voice because something is wrong
'Get a doctor!' they cried.

scream
to cry out loudly because you are excited, frightened or angry
The witch turned and all the children in the audience screamed out loud.

scream

shout
to speak as loud as you can
No need to shout! I can hear you!

shriek
a short, high cry
We all shrieked and clapped when our team won.

In other words

to call a spade a spade (idiom)
to tell the truth about something, even if it is not very polite
She is very direct and just calls a spade a spade.

WORD PLAY

Can you understand this text message?

Call me L8R–K8

Answer: Call me later – Kate

yell
to speak in a loud voice, usually because you are angry
They were yelling so loudly, we could hear them from outside.

● **to ask someone to come to a place**

summon
to order someone to be somewhere
The police summoned the witness to the court.

● **to telephone**

ring/phone
to telephone (informal)
Ring me later, will you?

● **to call someone or something a name**

name
to give someone a special name
What are you going to name the kitten?

a b **c** d e f g h i j k l m

Carry

bring · fetch · haul · lift · lug · support · take · tote · transport

● **to carry someone or something**

bring
to take something to the person speaking
Bring your homework to my house and we'll work on the essay together.

fetch
to go somewhere to get something and then bring it back
Our dog is good at fetching sticks.

fetch

lift
to raise something in the air
We lifted the baby out of his pram.

lug
to carry something, especially something heavy
We lugged a big bag of newspapers around all the houses.

support
to hold something up
They supported the stone blocks on wooden logs and rolled them along.

take
to carry something in a direction away from the person speaking
Take your jacket, it's going to rain.

tote
to carry something, especially something awkward or large
You can take it, but you'll have to tote it around all day.

In other words

to carry the weight of the world on your shoulders
(idiom)
to feel very worried or sad about things
She looks so worried — as if she has the weight of the world on her shoulders.

haul
to drag or pull something heavy
It took four men to haul the box around the corner.

haul

transport
to take goods from one place to another
New cars are transported on special lorries.

brainy · bright · cunning · intellectual · intelligent
knowledgeable · quick · smart · streetwise

good at learning or thinking

brainy (informal)
intelligent and good at studying
*Our last teacher liked brainy kids who got all the
answers right.*

bright
used to talk about someone who is
intelligent and clever
George is one of the brightest pupils.

bright

intelligent
good at learning and understanding things
You need to be very intelligent to be a doctor.

quick
able to understand things very quickly
She has a quick mind and can do sums in her head.

smart
someone who is able to solve problems or who
learns easily
That's a great idea! You're so smart!

In other words

a brain box (idiom)
someone who is very intelligent
*She's a bit of a brain box — she won the
school quiz.*

> **The opposites of
> clever are foolish
> and unintelligent.**

having a lot of knowledge or information

intellectual
educated in subjects that need to be studied for
a long time
The discussion was very intellectual.

knowledgeable
knowing a lot about a subject
The librarian is knowledgeable about a lot of things.

good at using your brain to get along

cunning
able to think and plan secretly so that you get
what you want
It was a cunning plan that almost worked.

streetwise
experienced in living in a city
The kids in that neighbourhood are pretty streetwise.

Did you know?

Clever has not always meant
'intelligent'. Until about 1700,
it meant 'expert at seizing'! We
think it originally comes from the
Norwegian word *klover* —
meaning ready or skilful.

● **something that is a little cold**

chilly
quite cold
Autumn is here and it's starting to get chilly.

cool
slightly cold
There's a nice, cool breeze down on the beach.

draughty
a draughty place has cold air blowing through it
My room is cold and draughty.

draughty

● **something that is very cold**

freezing
below the temperature at which water freezes
Polar bears live in freezing conditions.

frosty
extremely cold
It was a clear, frosty morning. There was ice on the windows.

> The opposite of cold is hot.

In other words

cool as a cucumber (idiom)
very relaxed under pressure
Dom is always as cool as a cucumber during exam time.

● **a person or an animal that is cold**

shivering
to be so cold (or frightened) that you shake slightly
The puppies were wet and shivering.

to have goosepimples or goosebumps
to be so cold (or frightened) that your skin raises up in little bumps
By the end of the walk we were covered in goosepimples.

goosepimples

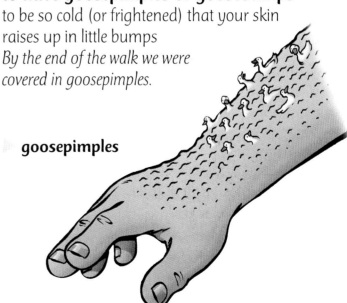

Different

● unlike something else

dissimilar
not the same
*The twins look the same
but their personalities
are dissimilar.*

diverse
used to talk about
many things being
different from each
other
*The menu has dishes
from diverse countries.*

not at all like
to say that something is
quite different from
something else
*Living in the country is not at all
like living in the city.*

● to be different
from everything else

distinctive
something that is easy to recognize because it is
different
The owl has a very distinctive call.

individual
a different way of doing something
*Every child has a special, individual way of being
creative.*

unique
very special or unusual, not like anything else
Climbing a mountain is a unique experience.

In other words

a one off (idiom)
a special or unusual thing or experience
Watching that spectacular sunset was a one off.

to be like chalk and cheese (idiom)
comparing two things that are completely different
Georgie and Katie are sisters but they're as different as chalk and cheese.

on a different wavelength (idiom)
to be thinking about something in very
different ways
*You and I are on different wavelengths
where music is concerned.*

● to differ

vary
to be different from each other thing in a group
The stones vary in size, shape and colour.

contrast with
to be obviously different from something else
*In contrast with the labrador, the Jack Russell is
very lively.*

**The opposite of
different is the
same.**

awkward · backbreaking · challenging · demanding · fiddly
gruelling · hard · impossible · strenuous · tough · tricky

● **not easy**

awkward
difficult in a way that makes people uncomfortable
My little sister is always asking awkward questions.

challenging
not easy but interesting or fun to work on
Writing a page for our school website is challenging.

demanding
needing hard work or a big effort
Being at school all day can be demanding for little children.

hard
not easy to understand or do
These sums are hard.

impossible
so difficult that it can't be done
It's impossible for me to meet you this afternoon.

tough
needing a lot of thought or work
Those exams are very tough.

The opposite of difficult is easy.
Look at easy for related words.

● **not easy to do because it is complicated**

tricky
full of problems
Decorating a birthday cake can be quite tricky.

tricky

fiddly
full of lots of small things or problems
This jigsaw is really fiddly.

● **not easy to do because it is physically hard**

backbreaking
needing a lot of physical work, especially lifting heavy things
Digging our vegetable garden was backbreaking work.

gruelling
tiring and difficult because it lasts a long time
In Victorian times, children worked long, gruelling hours in factories.

strenuous
needing a lot of physical effort
Cross country skiing is a strenuous sport.

In other words

to make a meal of something (idiom)
to pretend that a job is more difficult than it really is so that people will notice
Don't make such a meal of it, just do it!

Drink

drain · gulp · guzzle · lap up · polish off · quench
sip · swallow · swig

drain
to drink the last drop of something
Luke drained his water bottle before he got back to camp.

gulp
to drink something very quickly in large mouthfuls
I was so thirsty I gulped the juice down.

guzzle
to drink a lot of something very quickly
We guzzled our fizzy drinks.

lap up
the way animals drink with their tongues
The kittens lapped up all the milk.

polish off
to finish drinking
something you like
*Hannah polished off all
the apple juice.*

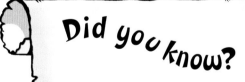

polish off

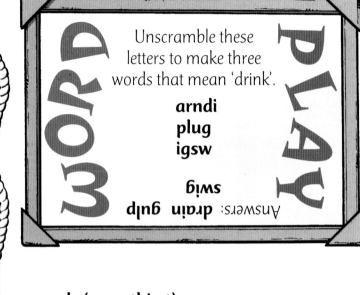

WORD PLAY

Unscramble these letters to make three words that mean 'drink'.

arndi
plug
igsw

Answers: drain gulp swig

quench (your thirst)
to drink something so that you stop being thirsty
We stopped halfway up the hill and quenched our thirst.

sip
to drink small mouthfuls of something
Just sip water when you've been running.

swig
to drink something in large mouthfuls
We walked around the funfair and swigged lemonade.

swallow
to make something go
down your throat
*This milk tastes so sour that
it's hard for me to swallow.*

swallow

Did you know?

The words 'lap', 'sip'
and 'drink' all come
from Old English.

easy

a breeze · a doddle · effortless · idiot-proof · painless
simple · straightforward · uncomplicated · user-friendly

● **not difficult to understand or do**

effortless
not easy, but made to look easy because someone does it well
Ballet dancers make dancing look effortless.

simple
easy to do or understand
She knew the answers so the test was simple.

straightforward
easy to do because it is clear what needs to be done
Putting the scooter together was pretty straightforward.

uncomplicated
easy to understand because there are not a lot of parts
Games for very small children need to be uncomplicated.

The opposite of easy is difficult.

● **easy to use**

idiot-proof
extremely easy to use
You can buy underwater cameras that are idiot-proof.

painless
not needing a lot of effort
Raising money for the school was painless.

user-friendly
clear and easy to use, especially to do with electronic things
This DVD is really user-friendly, even Dad can program it easily.

user-friendly

a breeze

● **easy to do**

a breeze
very easy to do (informal)
The girls were much better so beating the boys was a breeze.

a doddle
very easy to do, especially things such as tests (informal)
The short words in the spelling test were a doddle.

In other words

a piece of cake (idiom)
something that is very easy to do
That puzzle was a piece of cake!

Eat

bolt · chew · consume · demolish · devour · gobble · feed
munch · nibble · scoff · snack

In other words

could eat a horse (idiom)
very hungry
What's for dinner? I could eat a horse!

● **to eat food**

chew
to grind food with your teeth so you can swallow it
This meat is hard to chew.

consume
eat (formal)
Once opened, this product should be consumed within two days.

feed
how animals eat
The panda feeds on bamboo.

munch   **munch**
to eat noisily
The people behind us were munching crisps all through the movie.

● **to eat quickly**

bolt
to eat food quickly because you are in a hurry
We bolted our lunch so we could get back to the game.

demolish
a funny way to say that someone ate all of something quickly
They demolished all the food at the party within fifteen minutes.

devour
to eat something quickly because you are very hungry
We devoured the picnic in minutes.

gobble
to eat quickly
We gobbled our breakfast and ran for the bus.

scoff
to eat something quickly and greedily (informal)
What! You scoffed the lot?

● **to eat a little**

nibble
to take small bites
Our rabbit nibbles at carrots and lettuce.

snack   **nibble**
a small meal or to eat a small meal
We had a snack when we got home because supper wasn't ready.

e   f

Fast

accelerate · brisk · dash · high speed · quick · quickly · rapid · rush
speedy · supersonic

brisk
fast and energetic
We had a brisk walk along the seafront.

quick
fast
It was a quick decision.

rapid
very fast
The team made good, rapid progress and finished in first place.

speedy
fast and successful (informal)
Wishing you a speedy recovery.

● **moving fast**

quickly
fast, usually for a short time
Walk past quickly!

● **to go fast**

accelerate
to go more quickly, usually in a vehicle
As he neared the finish line, the driver accelerated.

dash
to move quickly or to leave a place quickly
They dashed out of the house to catch the bus.

dash

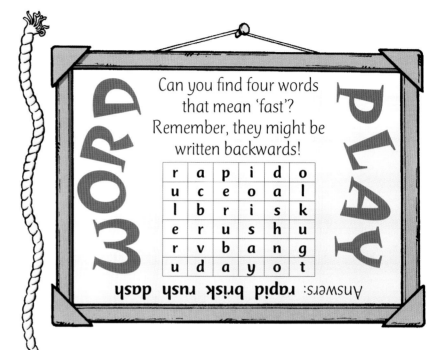

WORD **PLAY**

Can you find four words that mean 'fast'? Remember, they might be written backwards!

r	a	p	i	d	o
u	c	e	o	a	l
l	b	r	i	s	k
e	r	u	s	h	u
r	v	b	a	n	g
u	d	a	y	o	t

Answers: rapid brisk rush dash

rush
to move quickly because you are in a hurry
There's no need to rush, we've got plenty of time.

● **capable of going fast**

high-speed
can move very fast
The dentist uses a high-speed drill.

supersonic
can move faster than the speed of sound
Concorde is a supersonic plane.

The opposite of fast is slow.

Friend

amiable · buddy · circle · companion · crowd · gang
hospitable · mate · neighbourly · pal · smarmy · sociable · warm

● **friend**

buddy (mate/pal)
friend
We're all very good mates.

companion
someone you spend a lot of time with
They are travelling companions.

Did you know?

Cockney rhyming slang started in East London in Victorian times. People say words that rhyme with the word they want to say, rather than saying the word they mean. Look at these:
apples and pears = stairs
plates of meat = feet
loaf of bread = head

● **a group of friends**

circle
the people you know
We have a big circle of friends.

crowd
a group of friends you go out and do things with
Do you want to come? A crowd of us are going.

gang
a group of friends that meet often (informal)
It's a nice gang of people.

● **friendly**

amiable
friendly and likeable
He's amiable and easy to get along with.

hospitable
friendly and welcoming
Her parents are very hospitable and always ask us if we want something to eat or drink.

neighbourly
friendly and helpful
The people next door are very neighbourly.

smarmy
polite and friendly but in a false way
I don't like him, he's smarmy.

sociable
friendly and out-going
Their family is very sociable, they have lots of parties.

warm
friendly and caring
Jemma is a sweet, warm girl.

In other words
china
mate
(Cockney rhyming slang)
This comes from 'china plate' which rhymes with mate.

Frightened

● frightened

afraid
feeling nervous or frightened of something
Are you afraid of spiders?

dreading
not wanting to do something because something bad may happen
I'm dreading the school play.

afraid

panic-stricken
so frightened that you can't think
People were panic-stricken when the earthquake started.

petrified
so frightened that you can't move
We were absolutely petrified.

scared
feeling worried that something bad will happen
We were so scared, we thought that someone was trying to break into the house.

terrified
very frightened of something dangerous or nasty
They were terrified and just ran without looking back.

● frightening

chilling
very frightening, sometimes in a cruel or dangerous way
It was a chilling thought.

hair-raising

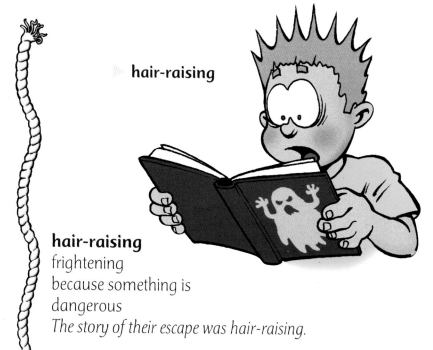

hair-raising
frightening because something is dangerous
The story of their escape was hair-raising.

scary
frightening
That Hallowe'en mask is too scary.

spooky
frightening in a strange way
The castle is really spooky at night.

In other words

scared of your own shadow (idiom)
always nervous and frightened
He's scared of his own shadow.

Funny

amusing · clown · comedian · comical · hilarious
humorous · light-hearted · witty

● **making you laugh**

amusing
funny and entertaining
Her stories are always amusing.

comical
funny in an unexpected way
Watching you try to catch the dog was really comical.

comical

hilarious
extremely funny
The jokes on that website are hilarious.

humorous
funny, entertaining and clever
This is a humourous book about a trip around the world.

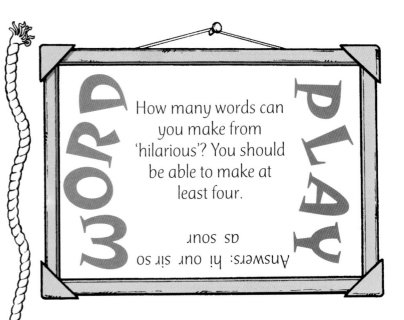

WORD PLAY

How many words can you make from 'hilarious'? You should be able to make at least four.

Answers: hi our sir so as sour

light-hearted
funny or poking fun in a gentle way
The programme is a light-hearted look at living on a farm.

witty
using words in a funny and entertaining way
Uncle Derek is very witty.

In other words

a good sense of humour
an ability to laugh and see the funny side of things
He's got a great sense of humour and is a lot of fun to be with.

can take a joke
able to laugh when people make fun of you
Oh, come on – can't you take a joke?

● **a person who is funny**

clown
a person whose job is to act silly and make people laugh
The clown at the circus had us all in stitches.

clown

comedian
a person whose job is to make people laugh
I want to be a comedian when I grow up.

f g

give

to give something to someone

donate
to give something to an organization or group
The company donated a computer to our school.

hand
to pass something from your hand to another person's hand
Hand me that book, will you?

pass on
to give someone information or papers
Thanks, I'll pass it on to the manager.

slip
to give someone something secretly
She slipped me a note as I walked past.

slip

to give someone something because of what they've done

award
to officially give someone a prize
They awarded the medals after the games.

present
to give someone something as part of a ceremony
The headmaster presented the prizes.

The opposite of give is take.

In other words

give and take (idiom)
a situation between two groups or people when each is allowed some of the things they want
Brothers and sisters have to give and take.

reward
to give someone something for being helpful
We rewarded the person who found our cat.

to give something to a group

distribute
to give something to a large group
The charity distributes medicine.

share out
to divide something into equal parts and give a part to each person in a group
We won a bag of sweets and shared them out among the team.

to arrange to give someone something after you die

bequeath
to officially arrange to give someone something after you die (formal)
They bequeathed the land to the tennis club.

good

amazing · brilliant · decent · excellent · fantastic · fun · great · impressive
incredible · lovely · marvellous · nice · outstanding · talented · wonderful

something you like or enjoy

amazing/incredible
something that is good in a surprising way
This DVD is amazing!

brilliant
very, very good
This website is brilliant!

excellent
extremely good
Their new CD is excellent.

fantastic/marvellous/wonderful
something good that makes you feel excited
The view from the top of the mountain is fantastic.

fun
enjoyable
This party game is fun.

great
very good or enjoyable
That ride is great! Let's go on it again.

lovely/nice
pleasant
Thank you, we've had a really nice time.

In other words

as good as gold
(idiom)
well behaved
Eliza has been as good as gold today.

> The opposite of good is bad.
> Also look at bad for related words.

something that is very well done or of high quality

impressive
something that is done to a high standard that you admire
That last goal was really impressive.

outstanding
something that is noticeably better than others
Einstein was an outstanding scientist.

outstanding

able to do something well

talented
naturally able to do something well
They made him captain because he is the most talented player.

morally good

decent
good and honest
Most people are decent and kind.

g h

Happy

● **feeling happy**

cheerful
happy most of the time
She's a cheerful, sunny person.

content
happy and satisfied in a quiet way
On a rainy day, I'm content sitting inside with a good book.

jolly
happy or enjoyable
Old King Cole was a jolly old soul.

In other words

over the moon (idiom)
very pleased about something
Mum got the job and she's over the moon.

Did you know?

The word 'happy' probably comes form an old Norse word, meaning chance or luck.

● **happy that something has happened**

delighted
very happy that something has happened
We're delighted to have won first place.

ecstatic
extremely happy and very excited that something has happened
The band was ecstatic when they won the award.

glad
happy that something has happened or changed
I'm so glad I found my mobile.

overjoyed
very happy about some good news
They were overjoyed when they heard the results.

pleased
happy and satisfied that something good has happened
Our teachers were pleased with the art exhibition.

thrilled
very excited and happy
She was thrilled with the presents.

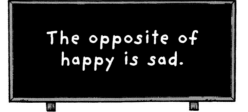

The opposite of happy is sad.

Hate

abhor · animosity · can't bear/stand · contempt · despise
detest · loathe

● to dislike or hate something

abhor
to strongly dislike or disapprove of something
(formal)
They abhor violence.

can't bear/stand
to dislike something so much that it upsets
you
Erggh! I can't bear scary movies.

can't bear

In other words

a pet hate (idiom)
something that you don't like at all because
it annoys you
Mobile phones are my teacher's pet hate.

despise
to strongly dislike something and think it is wrong
We despise racism.

detest
to strongly dislike or hate something or someone
Unfairness is something everybody detests.

loathe
to strongly dislike
something
*Some people
loathe cabbage.*

loathe

● a feeling of hating something or
someone

animosity
a feeling of angry hatred
There is animosity between the two groups.

contempt
a feeling of hatred about something that you
think is worthless
She holds the bullies in utter contempt.

The opposite of
hate is love.

h

Hot

balmy · baking · boiling · lukewarm · muggy · roasting · scalding · spicy · sweltering · warm

● not cold

lukewarm
only slightly warm (liquid or food)
The bathwater isn't really hot, just lukewarm.

scalding
very hot (liquid or steam)
Careful, that water is scalding!

warm
a temperature between hot and cool
Are you warm enough?

● hot (weather or places)

baking
very hot and dry
It's baking on the beach.

balmy
pleasantly warm
The weather is surprisingly balmy for the time of year.

boiling
very hot and uncomfortable
It's boiling in here, open a window.

muggy
hot and damp
Muggy weather sometimes makes you feel tired.

roasting
very hot and uncomfortable
I'm roasting in this sleeping bag.

roasting

> The opposite of hot is cold.

sweltering
very hot and damp
It was sweltering on sports day.

● hot (food)

spicy
tasting hot
Do you like very spicy curry?

sweltering

In other words

hot air (idiom)
when someone is full of hot air, they say things that they don't mean or don't really know
Their promises turned out to be so much hot air.

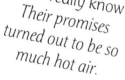

Imagine

conceive of
to invent something, like a plan or an idea
He conceived of the idea when he was very young.

daydream
to spend time imagining nice things so that you
forget about what you are doing or where you are
Stop daydreaming and pay attention, James!

dream of
to imagine something good that you want
to happen
*She's always dreamed
of having a horse.*

fantasize
to imagine
something that
probably won't
happen
*Mum and Dad fantasize
about what they'll do
when they win
the lottery.*

fantasize

Word partners

a vivid imagination
a powerful ability to imagine things
*My older sister has a very vivid
imagination.*

WORD PLAY

Unscramble the letters of
these words and place
them in alphabetical order.
1. retucip **2.** ese
3. yaderdma
4. aicnetulalh

Answers: **1.** picture
2. see **3.** daydream
4. hallucinate

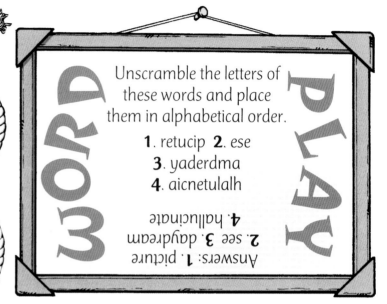

hallucinate
to believe that you
can see things
that aren't
really there
*Sometimes
when you have
a high fever,
you hallucinate.*

picture
to have a picture
of something in
your mind
*I know who you
mean but I can't
picture his face.*

picture

see
to have a picture of something in your mind
I can just see you in that jacket.

visualize
to get a clear picture of something in your mind
I'm sorry, I can't visualize what you mean.

i

Important

central

central
main
Peter Pan is the central character in the play.

critical
extremely important to the success of something
Finishing on time is critical.

crucial
important because other things depend on it
The support of parents is crucial.

essential
important to the highest degree
It is essential we leave on time tonight.

historic
so important that it will cause something to be remembered as part of history
It was a historic decision.

key
important to what will happen
Hard work is a key factor.

The opposite of important is unimportant.

major
one of the most important
Edinburgh is a major Scottish city.

notable
important and deserving attention
A notable feature of the school is the sports centre.

significant
having an important effect
It is a significant win.

vital
very important and necessary
Your help is vital.

weighty
important and serious
These are weighty questions.

weighty

In other words

VIP (abbreviation)
Very Important Person
They treated us like VIPs.

Job

assignment · chore · duty · errand · mission · occupation · profession · project · task · trade · undertaking · vocation

assignment
a piece of work that
someone gives you
*The assignment is to write
a 600 word essay.*

chore
a boring job
you have to
do often
*Feeding the pets
isn't really a chore, it's fun.*

assignment

duty
something that you have a responsibility to do
At scout camp, everyone has duties.

errand
a small job
While you're out, will you run some errands for me?

mission
an important job that someone goes somewhere
to do
The mission is to bring back the secret formula.

project
an important piece of work that needs planning
This is a long-term project.

task
a piece of work
*Each person is given a task so that the work gets done
more quickly.*

undertaking
a big and
important job
*Raising money
for a new
sports hall is
a huge
undertaking.*

● **jobs that
people do to
earn money**

In other words

**A job worth doing is
worth doing well.**
(proverb)

occupation
a person's full-time job
His occupation is police officer.

profession
a job that you need special training to do
Professions are jobs such as lawyer or doctor.

trade
a skilled job that you use your hands to do
Electrician, builder and furniture maker are all trades.

vocation
a job that you do because you feel strongly about
doing it
Teaching and nursing are vocations.

WORD PLAY

Unscramble the letters
to find four words that
mean 'job'.

1. ktsa **2.** reoch
3. rrndea **4.** uytd

Answers: **1.** task **2.**
chore **3.** errand
4. duty

j

Joke

gag
a short joke
The comedian had some good gags.

practical joke
a carefully planned joke
My brother played a practical joke on his best friend.

prank
a silly trick that isn't supposed to hurt anyone
We pulled a few pranks on Hallowe'en.

pun
a play on words that sound the same but mean something else
a pun: Why was six scared of seven? Because seven eight nine!

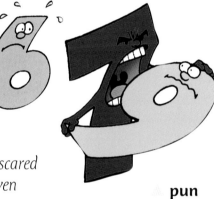

pun

punch line
the last line of a joke that makes it funny
Mum loves to tell jokes but she always forgets the punch line.

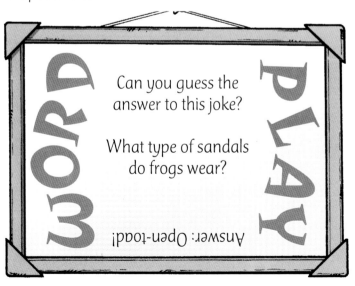

WORD PLAY

Can you guess the answer to this joke?

What type of sandals do frogs wear?

Answer: Open-toad!

In other words

to pull someone's leg (idiom)
to tell someone something that isn't true as a joke
I think Joe was pulling your leg, there isn't a frog in the bath.

riddle
a strange or difficult question that usually has a funny answer
Not all riddles are jokes.

wisecrack
a funny, clever remark
He's full of wisecracks!

wisecrack

in jest
said to make people laugh
It was said in jest – he didn't really mean it!

to be joking/kidding
not serious
I was only joking, I didn't really forget your birthday!

Jump

bound

to move quickly with big jumps
Kangaroos bound across the bush.

hop

to jump on one leg
The first part of the race is hopping for 25 metres.

hurdle

to jump over something while you are running
They hurdled the fence.

leap

to jump a long way
It was a huge leap from one ledge to the next.

pounce

pounce

to jump to catch something
The cat pounced on the mouse.

Word partners

jump at
to eagerly take the opportunity to do something
He jumped at the chance of going to the party.

skip

to go forward with small, quick jumps
We tried to skip all the way to school but we got too tired.

spring

to jump suddenly and quickly
The cheetah seemed to spring from nowhere.

spring

vault

to jump over something
The thief vaulted over the wall.

vault

In other words

jump the gun (idiom)
do something too soon
Now, don't jump the gun. Let's just think about this a bit more.

jump to conclusions (idiom)
to decide what you think about something before you know all the facts
I'm not to blame! Why do you always jump to conclusions about me?

j k

Know

to know something

appreciate
to understand that a situation is difficult or important
Do you appreciate how serious this is?

be aware of
to know about something
Are you aware of the new rule?

be familiar with
to know about something
We're familiar with the area, we went there on holiday last year.

be well-up on
to be well-informed and up to date about a subject
He's well-up on footballers.

In other words

to know something like the back of your hand (idiom)
to know something very well
I know this wood like the back of my hand.

feel
to know something through your feelings
You could feel the tension in the room.

realize
to notice or understand something you didn't before
I didn't realize it was so late.

feel

sense
to have the feeling that you know something even though there is no proof
They sensed something in the room.

a person who knows about something

expert
someone who knows a lot about a subject
You can ask experts questions on the Internet.

specialist
someone who has studied a subject very carefully and knows a lot about it
She's a specialist in Chinese medicine.

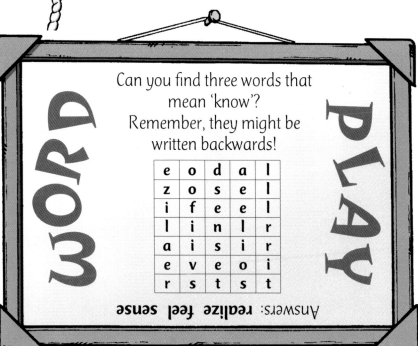

WORD PLAY

Can you find three words that mean 'know'?
Remember, they might be written backwards!

e	o	d	a	l
z	o	s	e	l
i	f	e	e	l
l	i	n	l	r
a	i	s	i	r
e	v	e	o	i
r	s	t	s	t

Answers: **realize feel sense**

Laugh

burst out laughing · cackle · chortle · chuckle · giggle · guffaw · roar with laughter · snigger · titter

● to laugh in a quiet way

giggle
to laugh in a silly, quiet way because something is funny or you are embarrassed
We couldn't stop giggling.

chuckle
to laugh quietly or to yourself
The cartoon made me chuckle.

● to laugh in a loud way because something is funny

burst out laughing
to laugh loudly and suddenly
We just looked at each other and burst out laughing.

guffaw
to laugh loudly in a way that is hard to control
We guffawed when she told us the joke.

roar with laughter
to laugh noisily and hard
The children roared with laughter.

The opposite of
laugh is cry.
Also look at cry for
related words.

Word partners

hearty laughter
enthusiastic, happy laughter

hollow laughter
laughter without feeling

● to laugh in an unpleasant way

cackle
to laugh loudly in a high voice
The witch cackled as she stirred the potion.

chortle
to laugh in a satisfied way, usually at or about someone else
They chortled as they played their trick.

snigger/titter
to laugh in an unkind way
Stop sniggering! Let's see if you can do any better!

In other words

to be in stitches (idiom)
to be laughing so hard that you can't stop
The jokes had us in stitches.

to roll in the aisles (idiom)
to be laughing hard at a funny film or performance
The audience was rolling in the aisles.

Look

examine · gaze · glance · glare · glimpse · inspect · peek · peep
peer · spot · spy · stare · study

● **to look at or see something quickly**

glimpse
to see someone or something for a very short time
I just glimpsed/caught a glimpse of that bird.

glance
to look at something or someone for
a short time
She glanced at her watch.

● **to notice or see something**

spot
to see or notice something or someone
We spotted a deer in the wood.

spy
to see or notice something or someone, usually
from a distance
We spied them coming up the street.

● **to look at someone or something
secretly**

peek
to look at something quickly and secretly
*They peeked at the presents
under the Christmas tree.*

peep
to look at something
for a short time, usually
when you don't want
anyone to see you
*Maddy peeped around
the corner.*

peep

glare

● **to look at something for a long time**

stare
to look directly at someone or something without
moving your eyes away
It's rude to stare.

glare
to stare angrily at someone or something
They glared at each other.

gaze
to look at someone or something for
a long time, usually with a good feeling
of love or pleasure
We gazed up at the stars in the sky.

● **to look at something or someone
carefully**

examine
to look at something very carefully, usually to
discover something
The scientists examined the fossils very closely.

inspect
to look at or check something very carefully,
especially to make sure it is safe or correct
They inspect all the tyres.

peer
to look carefully at something, usually because
you can't see it very well
They peered into the cave.

study
to look at something carefully, usually to learn or
understand something
Study the map closely, we don't want to get lost!

Loud

blaring · booming · deafening · ear-splitting/shattering
noisy · penetrating · piercing · rowdy · thunderous

● **very loud**

blaring
making a loud noise
The song starts with blaring horns and loud drums.

booming
very loud and deep
We could hear Joe's booming voice from outside.

deafening
so loud that you can't hear anything else
The explosion was deafening.

thunderous
extremely loud
When the music stopped, the applause was thunderous.

● **unpleasantly loud**

ear-splitting/ shattering
so loud that it hurts your ears
The fire alarm is ear-splitting.

ear-splitting

In other words

Sometimes we use 'loud' to describe things such as clothes that are unpleasantly colourful.

noisy
loud in an unpleasant way
It's noisy in the swimming pool today.

penetrating
loud, clear and unpleasant
The ship's horn gives out a penetrating blast.

piercing
loud and high-pitched
She's got a piercing voice, it went straight through me.

piercing

rowdy
people who are noisy and badly behaved
A few of them were rowdy but most were just having fun.

○Word partners

Loud and clear
something that is obvious and easy to understand
We understood the message loud and clear.

The opposites of loud are soft and low.

36

1

Love

● **to love someone**

be fond of
to like someone very much
They're very fond of each other.

be close to
to love someone you can talk to easily
I'm very close to my older sister.

care about
to feel concerned about and like someone
We care about all children, everywhere.

△ **be close to**

● **to love someone or something very much**

adore
to really love someone or something
Molly adores chocolate.

be devoted to
to love and be loyal to someone
My grandparents are devoted to each other.

worship
to love or admire someone very much
He worships the basketball team!

△ **adore**

Word partners

fall in love
to become very fond of someone or something

love at first sight
to fall in love immediately

● **feeling or showing love**

affectionate
showing love
Our baby brother is very sweet and affectionate.

doting
showing love by paying a lot of attention to someone
They are doting grandparents.

tender
gentle and loving
She gave the children a tender look.

The opposite of love is hate.

Make

assemble
to put together the parts of something
We have to assemble the desk from a kit.

build
to make something by putting parts together
They're building a clubhouse for kids only.

concoct
to make something strange to eat or drink
The wizard concocted a magic potion.

concoct

create
to make something that wasn't there before
Our class created a sculpture for the park.

fashion
to make something to do a particular job
The castaway fashioned a sail for the raft.

WORD PLAY

Unscramble the letters to find four words that mean 'make'.

1. ldbiu   2. eearct
3. nfoaish   4. cccootn

Answers: 1. build 2. create 3. fashion 4. concoct

form
to make (or be a part of) something
Water is formed from hydrogen and oxygen.

generate
to make something by using a process
The power station generates electricity.

manufacture
to make something, especially in a factory
They manufacture toys.

mould
to shape a substance, such as clay
The wax is moulded into candles.

produce
to make something
Many plants produce flowers in the spring.

In other words

cobble something together (idiom)
to make something roughly and quickly
We didn't have a real go-cart but we cobbled something together.

The opposite of make is destroy.

m

Mistake

blunder · error · fault · gaffe · goof · oversight · slip
mix-up · misjudge

● **a mistake**

blunder
a stupid or clumsy mistake
It was a foolish blunder.

error
a serious mistake you don't know you're making
They made an error with our bill.

fault
a mistake (that someone is to blame for)
Sorry, that was my fault.

gaffe
an embarrassing mistake
*Putting sugar on your eggs in the restaurant was
a real gaffe.*

oversight
a mistake you make by forgetting or not noticing
something
*Everyone should have been invited — leaving their
names off was an oversight.*

slip
a small mistake
that is easy to
correct
*It was just a slip of
the tongue.*

In other words

**put your foot
in it** (idiom)
to say something
stupid or secret that
you shouldn't
have said
*You really put your
foot in it when you
mentioned the
surprise party!*

● **to make a mistake**

goof
to make a silly mistake
I goofed the answer.

misjudge
to make a mistake by deciding to do the
wrong thing
They misjudged the situation.

mix-up
to make a mistake that confuses things
*We were supposed to play the match
yesterday but we mixed-up the dates.*

slip

Money

allowance · cash · change · coins · currency · figure
fortune · pocket money · sum · wealth

cash
notes and coins used as money
Do you have any cash with you?

change
money that you get back when you pay for
something
Count your change.

coins
small pieces of metal used as money
Some machines only take coins, not notes.

currency
the type of money that is used in a country
*The dollar is the currency in Canada, the USA and
Australia.*

● **a lot of money**

a fortune
a very large amount of money
Great idea! We'll make a fortune!

wealth
a large amount of money or possessions
*The king lived in a castle and had great wealth,
but he was lonely.*

Did you know?

The word 'money' probably
comes from *Moneta*, a name
given to the Roman goddess
Juno, whose temple was used to
store valuable things.

In other words

money doesn't grow on trees
(idiom)
often used if money is in short supply, or to
explain that you should spend money wisely
*No, you can't have a new bike — money doesn't
grow on trees you know!*

● **amounts of money**

figure
an exact amount of money
The figure is £34.98.

sum
an amount of money
It was a tidy sum, but he didn't say how much.

● **money that someone gives another
person**

allowance
money someone gets regularly, not for working
The allowance covers basic living expenses.

pocket money
money children get from their parents each week
*I work for my dad on Saturday mornings to earn
pocket money.*

m

Move

budge · relocate · shift · squirm · stir · swing · transfer
transport · wriggle · writhe

budge
to move a little way
This is stuck, it won't budge.

relocate
to move something permanently to another place
We're moving house – Dad's firm has relocated to another city.

shift
to move from one place to another
Can you help me shift this over to the other side of the room?

transfer
to move from one place to another
The player transferred to another team.

transport
to take people or goods from one place to another
The new cars are transported by rail.

● **people or animals moving their bodies**

stir
to move slightly
She stirred in her sleep but didn't wake up.

stir

In other words

move heaven and earth (idiom)
to do everything that you possibly can to make something happen or stop it from happening
I moved heaven and earth to get you tickets.

squirm
to move your body from side to side because you are uncomfortable
Stop squirming and sit still.

swing
to move through the air
Monkeys swing from tree to tree.

wriggle
to move your body this way and that to get through a small space
We wriggled through the rocks and into the cave.

writhe
to move your body in big, sudden movements
The dancers writhed across the stage.

41

Name

alias · brand name · code name · identity · initial · maiden name
namesake · nickname · pen name · pseudonym

● people's names

identity
a person's name
The police are keeping his identity a secret.

initial
the first letter of each of your names
Her initials are BJH.

maiden name
a married woman's surname before she was married
These days, many women keep their maiden names after they get married.

namesake
a person who has the same name as you, especially a famous person
Our dog's namesake is Beckham.

nickname
a name your friends or family call you
Bizzy isn't her real name, it's a nickname.

namesake

● false names

alias
a different name someone is known by, especially a criminal
He was living here under an alias.

Did you know?

'Anonymous' is a name that people use if they don't want people to know their real name. It is also the name that people put at the end of poems, quotes, stories and plays when they don't know who wrote them. It comes from the Greek words *an* = without and *onyma* = name.

pen name
another name writers use instead of their own names
Mark Twain is the pen name of Samuel Clemens.

pseudonym
a name used by someone instead of their real name
Singers and actors sometimes use pseudonyms.

pen name

● names for things

brand name
the name a company gives a product
Playstation ® is a brand name.

code name
a secret name for someone or something
His code name is Storm Cloud.

Near

close · handy · local · nearby · neighbouring · next
surrounding · in the vicinity · within walking distance

close
very near
The swimming pool is close to our school.

handy
conveniently near
The shop is just around the corner from our house, which is handy.

in the vicinity
in the area around a place (formal)
Police believe the thief is still in the vicinity.

local
near a place, in an area
Can you tell me where the local post office is?

in the vicinity

nearby
near where you are
Is there a leisure centre nearby?

neighbouring
near the place where you live or the place you are talking about
The secondary school is in the neighbouring village.

next
the one that is closest
My best friend lives in the house next door.

next

> ### The opposite of near is far.

surrounding
near and around a place
There are two supermarkets in the surrounding area.

within walking distance
close enough to walk to easily
We have a cinema within walking distance of our house.

In other words

on your doorstep (idiom)
very near the place where you live
Some people like living in cities because everything is on your doorstep.

New

brand new
completely new
We've bought a brand new car.

fresh
clean, new and not used
The tennis players asked for fresh balls.

innovative
new, different and better
The skateboard is an innovative design.

just out
very new
It's just out on CD.

The opposite of new is old.

brand new

latest
the most recent
This is the latest version of the game.

newcomer
a person who has recently arrived in a place
The family are newcomers to our neighbourhood.

novel
new, interesting and different
Our teacher said having hot drinks at break was a novel idea.

recent
made or done a short time ago
We are looking for recent articles about the zoo.

original
new, not done before
That painting is an original, not a print.

pioneering
done for the first time
Marie Curie did pioneering research.

In other words

hot off the press (idiom)
the latest news
This is the news from the Olympics – hot off the press.

things that are old

ancient
extremely old, existing many years ago
Archimedes was a scientist in ancient Greece.

▲ ancient

antique
old and valuable
My grandfather gave me an antique pocket watch.

second-hand
owned by someone else before you buy it
Charity shops sell second-hand clothes.

used
not new, or owned by someone else before
Used computers are advertised in the local newspaper.

vintage
old and one of the best of its type
Vintage wine is very expensive.

people who are old

ageing
becoming older
The UK has an ageing population.

> The opposites of old are new and young.

In other words

as old as the hills (idiom)
very old
Aw! That joke is as old as the hills.

elderly
old (polite)
Gran is quite elderly but she still likes to go cycling with us.

be getting on
getting older
Grandad is getting on a bit.

▲ elderly

veteran
old and experienced
Dad plays on the veteran team.

things or places for people who are old

geriatric
to do with old people
Medical studies of the elderly are called geriatric medicine.

force

to open something that is stuck or locked by pushing hard on it
The firefighters forced the lift doors open.

pick a lock

to open a lock with something that is not a key
Car locks are extra safe so thieves can't pick the locks.

prise

to force something apart to open it
The trunk was prised open.

prise

unbolt

to open a door or gate by sliding a metal bar across
Carefully unbolt the door and lead the pony out.

unfold

to open paper or cloth and spread it out
Unfold the map and try to find out where we are.

unlock

to open a lock using a key
Can you unlock the door? My hands are full.

Word partners

an open mind

Not decided in advance
I have an open mind about the holiday.

Did you know?

We sometimes use 'open' to describe people who are honest and happy to talk about things.

unscrew

to take the top off a container by turning it
If you can't unscrew something, try using a cloth to hold it.

unwrap

to open a parcel by taking paper or cloth off it
We unwrap our presents on Christmas morning.

to be open

ajar

slightly open
If the door is ajar, just go straight in.

wide open

completely open
We left the garage door wide open by mistake.

ajar

> The opposites of open are close and closed.

average
typical, like most others of the same type
An average lesson lasts 45 minutes.

banal
ordinary, not interesting or new
Some people think the words in pop songs are banal.

bland
boring, dull or not tasty
Bland foods are not spicy.

everyday
not unusual or special
The Internet is a part of everyday life now.

mundane
ordinary and dull
Cleaning the rabbit's cage is a mundane task.

mundane

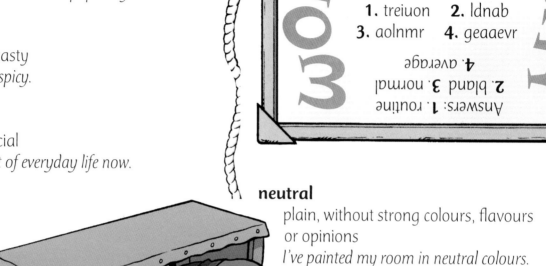

WORD PLAY

Unscramble the letters to find four words that mean 'ordinary'.

1. treiuon   2. ldnab
3. aolnmr   4. geaaevr

Answers: 1. routine
2. bland 3. normal
4. average

neutral
plain, without strong colours, flavours or opinions
I've painted my room in neutral colours.

normal
like other people or things of the same type
His height is normal for his age.

routine
usual and done frequently
I see the dentist twice a year for a routine check-up.

standard
usual
The printer uses a standard cartridge.

In other words

as dull as dishwater (idiom)
to be very ordinary and rather boring
This film is as dull as dishwater.

The opposites of ordinary are special and extraordinary.

o

Part

bit
a small part
Would you like a bit of this chocolate bar?

branch
an office or shop that is part of a big organization
Mum works in the local branch of the bank.

component
part of a machine or system
The hard disk is a component of computers.

cross-section
a part of something that is cut or divided to show
how the rest works or looks
This cross-section shows the different layers of skin.

crumb
a small bit of bread or cake
Who ate all the cake? There are only crumbs left!

crumb

element
one of the separate parts of something
*Different levels are an important element of any good
computer game.*

> **The opposites of
> part are whole
> and all.**

In other words

part and parcel
(idiom)
a necessary part of
something
*Homework is part and
parcel of being at
school.*

fraction
a small part of an amount or number
We've only raised a fraction of the amount we need.

ingredient
part of a food recipe
Mix all the ingredients together.

portion
part of something larger
A portion of the profits goes to charity.

section
a part of something that is separate from
something else
Which section of the school is your classroom in?

segment
a part of something such as fruit
*Divide the orange into segments before you put it in
the fruit salad.*

Payment

● **payment for work or service**

bonus
extra money for working hard
Dad got a bonus for getting a new account.

fee
the amount of money paid for something
The school fees are high.

salary
the total payment someone gets each year for doing a job
Mum's salary is higher now that she has a new job.

wages
the money that someone gets each week for doing a job
Wages are paid every Thursday.

● **payment in a restaurant**

tip
money that you give a waiter for service
Are you going to leave a tip?

tip

● **payment as a punishment**

fine
an amount of money a person pays for breaking the law
We had to pay a parking fine.

Did you know?
'Pay' comes from the Latin word *pacare* which means 'to please, pacify or satisfy'. It meant this in England until about 1500.

bribe
payment to a person so that they will do something, usually illegal
The prisoner gave the guard a bribe.

deposit
a payment you make when you decide to buy something, to prove that you will buy it
I put a £10 deposit down on the bike.

instalment
a partial payment that you make to buy something over a period of time
I paid instalments every month.

refund
money that you get back when you return something, usually to a shop
We got a full refund on the television.

In other words
pay through the nose (idiom)
pay too much for something
You have to pay through the nose for some trainers.

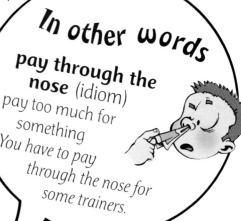

p

Person

family
a group of people who are related
How many kids are there in your family?

folks (informal)
people
They're friendly folks.

individual
one person
Every classroom is made up of unique individuals.

human/human being
a man, woman or child
The gorillas are not used to seeing humans.

family

humanity
all the people who have ever lived
Cave paintings are early records of humanity.

kin
members of a family
Next of kin means the person you are most closely related to.

somebody/someone
a person – used when you do not know the person's name or when it is not important to use their name
Quick, somebody call an ambulance!

● people in a story

character
a person in a book, film, game or story
Who is your favourite character?

hero/heroine
the main character in a story, or a person who does something brave
The hero killed the dragon.

WORD PLAY

Unscramble the letters to find four family members.

1. ousinc **2.** ceine
3. uelnc **4.** nweehp

Answers: **1.** cousin
2. niece **3.** uncle
4. nephew

humankind
all the people in the world
This is something for all humankind to be proud of.

In other words
person in the street (idiom)
ordinary people
We say 'the man or woman in the street' to talk about what most people think. Sometimes we say 'Joe Public' to talk about an average person.

Poor

broke · deprived · destitute · disadvantaged · impoverished
needy · penniless · underprivileged

broke
not having any money temporarily (informal)
I can't go with you, I'm broke this week.

deprived
not having the things you need for a normal life
Charles Dickens had a deprived childhood.

destitute
so poor that you do not have basic things such as enough food
The refugees are destitute.

Did you know?

The word 'poor' dates back to the 13th century. It comes from the Old French *povre* and the Latin *parere*.

disadvantaged
not having the same opportunities as other people
The charity helps disadvantaged familes.

impoverished
made poor
The country was impoverished after years of drought.

needy
not having enough money
Anyone who is needy is welcome to come and eat.

The opposite of poor is rich.

penniless
without any money
The winning lottery ticket was found by a penniless beggar.

penniless

underprivileged
poor and with fewer opportunities than other people
We collect aluminium cans to raise money for underprivileged families.

In other words

as poor as church mice (idiom)
very poor
My grandparents were as poor as church mice when they first came to this country.

p

Pretend

artificial · bluff · fake · false · impersonate · imposter
insincere · make-believe · masquerade · pose as

● to pretend

bluff
to pretend that you know something or that you
will do something
You're bluffing!

impersonate
to pretend that you are someone else
He was arrested for impersonating a policeman.

masquerade
to dress up in a disguise
They masqueraded as children.

pose as
to pretend to be someone else
She was posing as the headmistress.

In other words

to cry crocodile tears (idiom)
to pretend to be upset
*Your crocodile tears
don't fool me.*

● not real

artificial
not real or not natural
The coats were made with artificial fur.

fake/false
something that pretends
to look similar to something else

*Are they false eyelashes you
are wearing?*

false

insincere
not meaning what you say
His apology sounded very insincere.

make-believe
not real
The film is just make-believe.

● people who pretend

impostor
a person who pretends to be someone else
*The story is about an impostor who pretends
to be king.*

Did you know?

In England in 1491, Perkin Warbeck
pretended to be one of the Princes in
the Tower, who had supposedly been
murdered by their uncle, Richard III.
King Henry VII eventually tracked
down the pretender, and he was
executed in 1499.

Problem

catch
a hidden problem
There is a catch for arriving late: you have to work through your lunch hour today.

complication
a problem that makes a situation more difficult
It will be on time unless there are complications.

difficulty
a problem that is not easy to deal with
I'm having difficulty choosing.

dilemma
a very difficult choice
We have a major dilemma – we can go out, but we have to take my little brother with us.

In other words

stumbling block (idiom)
a problem that is likely to stop someone from doing what they want to do
The time limit may be a stumbling block.

hassle
an annoying problem (informal)
We had a bit of hassle getting the dog into the car.

hassle

hiccup
a small problem that is quickly solved (informal)
There was a minor hiccup but nothing serious to worry about.

hindrance
something that stops you from doing something easily
I was trying to wash our car but the rain was a real hindrance.

hindrance

hurdle
a problem that you have to solve so that you can do what you are trying to do
The team has had to overcome several hurdles: injuries, player moves and lack of funds.

snag
a difficulty (informal)
The snag is, tickets are very expensive.

p

Promise

● to make a promise

assure
to say that something is true or that something will happen to make someone feel better
The vet assured us that there was nothing to worry about.

give your word (of honour)
to make a very serious promise
He gave his word that he would never do it again.

guarantee
to say that something is true or that something will happen because you are very sure about it
I guarantee there won't be any more problems.

pledge
to say that you will do something or give something
We pledged £5 for the sponsored walk.

swear
to make a very serious promise that something is true, sometimes officially
Do you swear to tell the truth?

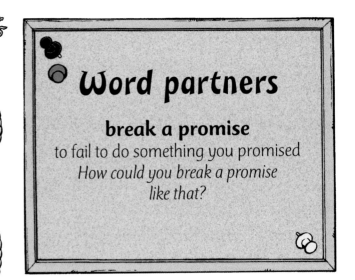

Word partners

break a promise
to fail to do something you promised
How could you break a promise like that?

undertake
an official or legal promise
The government has undertaken to reduce poverty.

vow
to make a serious promise or decision
We vowed that we would be friends forever.

● to fulfil a promise

deliver
to do what you promised
Will they be able to deliver what they promised?

stand by/stick to
to keep a promise even though the situation has changed
They said they would stand by the promise.

go through with
to keep a promise, especially if you no longer want to/think you can
We don't think we can win the match but we're going to go through with it anyway.

In other words

promise the earth (idiom)
to promise something that is impossible

My brother promised us the earth if we would just be quiet.

Proud

arrogant · bigheaded · boastful · conceited · haughty
pompous · smug · snobbish · superior · vain

arrogant
overly proud of yourself, acting as though you are more important than other people
He is arrogant and rude.

bigheaded
feeling that you are very clever, especially because you have been successful at something
Since Jemma was made head girl, she's acting really bigheaded.

bigheaded

boastful
talking proudly about things you have or have done
He can't open his mouth without being boastful.

conceited
overly proud of your abilities, looks or the things you have done
It's difficult to be friends with a conceited person.

haughty
proud and unfriendly
I thought she was haughty but she's really just shy.

pompous
trying to impress people with how important you are
It was a pompous speech.

> The opposite of proud is ashamed.

In other words
too big for your boots
(idiom)
believing that you are more important than you really are
You're getting too big for your boots. You can't tell me what to do!

smug
too pleased with yourself
He won't be so smug when he finds out that he came second this time.

snobbish
thinking that you are better than someone else because you are in a higher social position
Snobbish people don't get on well at our school.

superior
thinking that you are better than other people
It's difficult to learn from people who think they are superior.

vain
thinking that you are very good-looking
Stop looking in the mirror, you vain thing!

vain

p

Put

apply · deposit · heap · lay · lean · pile · place · position
prop · stack · stand

apply

to put a liquid such as paint on something
Apply a thin layer and allow to dry completely.

deposit

to put something down somewhere
He deposited the book on the table with a thump.

deposit

lay

to put something down flat on a surface
Lay the coats on the bed, please.

place

to put something somewhere carefully
Place the stencil in the centre of the paper.

position

to carefully move something into a certain position
Position the prism so that the light shines through it.

● to put something against something else

lean

to put something against a wall or other vertical surface
Lean the ladder against the wall.

prop

to lean something against something else for support
I'll prop my bike against the wall.

stand

to lean something against a wall so that it is nearly vertical
Stand the picture in the corner for a minute.

● to put things on top of one another

heap

to throw or drop things on top of each other in an untidy way
He just heaps his clothes in the middle of the floor.

pile

to put things on top of each other
Pile the books on the table.

heap

stack

to put things carefully on top of one another
The CDs are stacked in the cupboard.

WORD PLAY

Can you find four words that mean 'put'? Remember, they might be written backwards!

a	p	e	s	x	l
i	r	o	s	b	p
t	o	n	t	r	e
r	p	l	a	c	e
e	e	a	n	s	n
s	e	y	d	l	e
a	b	i	o	r	u

Answers: **prop lay stand place**

56

Quiet

hushed
quiet on purpose
The conversation in the waiting room was hushed.

inaudible
so quiet that you cannot hear it
He spoke in an almost inaudible whisper.

low
quiet and deep
There was a low hum coming from the machine.

muffled
quiet and unclear or blurred
Their speech is muffled by the helmets they are wearing.

muffled

muted
quieter than usual
We could hear muted voices in the corridor.

silent
with no sound
Please be absolutely silent while we are recording.

soft
quiet and pleasant
There is soft music on in the background.

In other words

as quiet as a mouse (idiom)
very quiet
I didn't hear you come in, you were as quiet as a mouse.

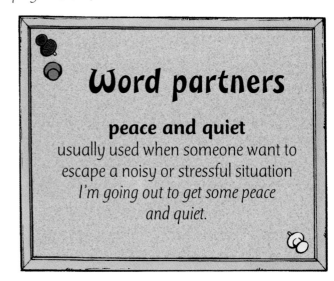

still
calm and quiet
The night was still and the sky was full of stars.

subdued
quieter than usual because you are sad or worried
You seem a bit subdued – are you okay?

taciturn
saying very little
He plays a stern, taciturn man.

The opposites of quiet are noisy and loud.

Word partners

peace and quiet
usually used when someone want to escape a noisy or stressful situation
I'm going out to get some peace and quiet.

p   q

Real

● **not false**

authentic
real or true
This is an authentic antique map.

bona fide
real and honest
Make sure it's a bona fide website before you buy anything online.

genuine
not a fake
Genuine leather lasts a long time.

true

true
not a lie
It's true. The dog really did eat my homework!

● **real feelings**

heartfelt
strong and truly meant
Please accept our heartfelt thanks.

sincere
real and truly felt
I trust her and think she is completely sincere.

> **The opposites of real are false and imaginary.**

In other words

the Real McCoy
(idiom)
the real thing, not a copy
Origin – This comes from an American boxer, Kid McCoy, who was called The Real McCoy.

● **existing, not imaginary**

actual
real
Her nickname is Posh but her actual name is Victoria.

concrete
based on facts
Do the police have any concrete evidence?

solid
based on real facts
There is solid evidence that smoking is bad for you.

concrete

Remember

● **to remember**

recall
to remember something on purpose
As I recall, we said we'd meet at the sports centre.

recollect
to be able to remember something
We went to Greece when I was a small child but I don't recollect anything about it.

relive
to remember something very clearly
I relived missing that goal many times.

relive

reminisce
to think or talk about nice things from the past
My parents like to reminisce about living in Africa.

● **to cause someone to remember**

prompt
to help someone remember something, especially an actor in a play
My job is to prompt the other children when they forget their lines.

remind
to make someone remember something they need to know or do
Remind me to leave a note for the milkman.

> The opposite of remember is forget.

● **easy to remember**

haunting
easy to remember in a mysterious way
The song has a beautiful, haunting melody that keeps going through my head.

haunting

memorable
easy to remember because it is very special
Meeting the prince was a memorable moment.

unforgettable
easy to remember because it affected you a lot
My first day at the new school was unforgettable.

In other words

something rings a bell (idiom)
something makes you partly remember something
James? The name rings a bell.

rack your brains (idiom)
try to remember something
Where are we going on holiday? I've been racking my brains trying to remember.

Rich

affluent
having a lot of money to buy things with
This is an affluent neighbourhood.

comfortable
having enough money
My grandparents saved money so they could have a comfortable retirement.

flush
having more money than you usually have (informal)
I'll treat you — I'm flush right now.

flush

prosperous
successful and having a lot of money
The town has become prosperous since the factory was built.

> The opposite of rich is poor.

wealthy
rich
They are a wealthy family and they're very generous.

well-heeled
having a lot of money and nice clothes (informal)
They look well-heeled.

well-off
having more money than most people
They've had problems but now they're quite well-off.

Did you know?

'Rich' comes from an Old English word *rice* — which meant wealthy, powerful or mighty.

In other words

to go from rags to riches (idiom)
to start life poor and become rich in later life
It's a rags to riches story.

to be rolling in it (idiom)
to be very rich
Most pop stars are absolutely rolling in it!

● people who are rich

the haves
people who have money
Unfortunately, there are still the haves and have-nots.

a man/woman of means
a person who is rich and has property
The racehorse owner is a man of means.

Right

accepted
approved or agreed that something is right
It is an accepted fact that the world is not flat.

accurate
completely correct and true
You have to type in web addresses accurately.

appropriate
right for a certain situation
It's not appropriate to wear pyjamas to school.

apt
exactly right or suitable for a situation
Several pupils made apt remarks during the discussion.

correct
with no mistakes ('correct' is more formal than 'right')
Use the key to check that your answers are correct.

fitting
suitable or right for a particular situation (formal)
The poem was a fitting end to the ceremony.

The opposite of right is wrong.

just
fair, morally right
It was a just punishment for the crime.

proper
right or correct
Put the books in the proper order.

In other words

to be in the right place at the right time (idiom)
to be in a place or a position where something good is offered
She's so lucky – always in the right place at the right time.

suitable
right for a particular situation or time
Trainers aren't suitable shoes to wear to a wedding.

suitable

WORD PLAY

Which of these statements is right? If you are unsure, look them up in an encyclopedia.

1. Paris is the capital city of France
2. *Triceratops* was a meat-eating dinosaur
3. The three states of matter are liquid, solid and steam

Answers: **1.** Yes **2.** Plant-eating **3.** Liquid, solid and gas

Run

bolt · dash · flee · gallop · jog · lope · race · rush · sprint · tear

bolt
to run or move quickly because you are frightened
The horse bolted when the bell rang.

bolt

dash
to run fast for a short distance
It was raining so we dashed to the car.

flee
to run away from danger
The children were fleeing from the monsters.

gallop
to run quickly with big steps
He galloped around the house.

jog
to run quite slowly for quite a long way
Mum jogs three times a week.

lope
to run with big, relaxed strides
The highjumper loped up to the bar and sprang over it.

race
to run fast, especially against someone in a competition
We raced against each other.

flee

rush
move quickly to get somewhere or do something in a hurry
Mum was rushing around the house looking for her keys.

sprint
to run as fast as you can
The winner sprinted across the finishing line.

tear
to run fast without watching where you're going
He tore around the corner of the building and straight into the teacher.

Word partners

run for cover
to move quickly to find shelter
As the rain began, we ran for cover.

race

sad

dejected · depressed · desolate · despondent · fed up · glum
homesick · low · down · miserable · unhappy

fed up
unhappy and annoyed or bored (informal)
I'm fed up waiting for you.

glum
sad-looking
Why the glum face?

homesick
sad because you are away from home and miss the people there
At first you'll feel homesick, but then you'll make new friends.

glum

down/low
sad and without energy
You might feel down when you have flu.

unhappy
sad because of something that happens
What's wrong? You look unhappy.

◉ very sad

dejected
sad and disappointed
We were dejected when we lost.

> **The opposite of sad is happy.**

In other words

sadder but wiser (idiom)
to have learned something from a bad or difficult experience
We came back from the match sadder but wiser.

depressed
feeling sad, usually for a long time
I was depressed when we first moved here but now I really like it.

desolate
extremely sad and lonely
It is a flat, desolate landscape.

despondent
very sad and disappointed or not hopeful about the future
The team is despondent — they haven't won a match all year.

miserable
extremely sad
When you feel miserable you should just get up and do something.

consistent
steady, staying the same
Jess has made consistent improvement this term.

word for word
using exactly the same words
She repeated his speech, word for word.

verbatim (formal)
in exactly the same words as the original
It is a verbatim account of the trial.

something that is the same as
something else

carbon copy
exactly like another thing
The puppies are carbon copies of their mother.

counterpart
someone who has the same position as
someone else
The ministers met their Canadian counterparts.

equivalent
something that has the same amount or size
as something else
What is the equivalent of £10 in euros?

identical
exactly the same
That jacket is almost identical to mine.

synonym
a word that means the same as another word
Sidewalk is the American synonym of pavement.

carbon copy

The opposite of
same is different.

Can you match the
words that mean
the same?

1. Part   a. Tale
2. Hot   b. Drowsy
3. Story   c. Roasting
4. Sleepy   d. Bit

Answers: 1d 2c 3a 4b

WORD PLAY

blurt out

to say something without thinking
He blurted out the answer.

blurt out

remark

to say what you think about something
The reporter remarked on our school's website.

tell

to say something to someone
Please don't tell anyone.

whisper

to say something very softly
You play the game by whispering the sentence to the person next to you.

comment

to give an opinion
The captain commented on each player's performance.

exclaim

to say something loudly or suddenly
'This ride is fantastic!' she exclaimed.

hint

to say something indirectly
Mr Hunt hinted that there would be a test.

mention

to say a little bit about a fact
The head mentioned that there would be new pupils this term.

mumble

to say something unclearly
Don't mumble when you're on stage, speak clearly.

mutter

to say something quietly, especially if you are complaining
One of the players muttered something about the referee.

whisper

In other words

it goes without saying (idiom)
so obvious that something does not actually have to be said
It goes without saying that he'll do a good job.

Secret

behind someone's back
done without telling someone
Friends don't do things behind your back.

cagey
not willing to tell other people your plans
(informal)
*Dad's being a bit cagey about where we're going
on holiday — he wants it to be a surprise.*

clandestine
secret, sometimes illegal
The group holds clandestine meetings.

concealed
not showing
The microphone was concealed in a lamp.

confidential
private
The report is confidential.

Word partners

keep a secret
to not tell anyone a secret someone
has told you
Can you keep a secret?

covert
done in a secret way
The agents are involved in covert operations.

furtive
in a secret way
It was a quick, furtive pass.

hidden
not shown or visible
There's a message hidden in the book.

hush-hush
very secret
*We don't know what they're planning, it's all very
hush-hush.*

in private
done where other people cannot see or hear
They will discuss it in private.

In other words

**between you, me and
the gatepost** (idiom)
what you say when you tell someone
something you don't want anyone
else to know
Now, this is just between you, me and the gatepost.

> The opposite of
> secret is public.

sleep

catnap · doze · drift off · drop off · hibernate · kip · nap
slumber · snooze

catnap
a very short sleep, usually not very deep
Why don't you have a quick catnap before we leave for the airport?

doze
to sleep lightly
I was just dozing in front of the TV.

drift off
to go to sleep slowly
Try to be quiet, we're hoping the baby will drift off.

drop off
to go to sleep easily
I was so tired after swimming that I dropped off as soon as my head hit the pillow.

drift off

In other words
to sleep like a log (idiom)
to sleep very well
*Did you get some sleep?
Yeah, I slept like a log!*

hibernate (for animals)
to go to sleep for the winter
Bears sometimes hibernate in caves.

kip (informal)
a short sleep
You'll be able to have a kip in the car.

> **The opposite of asleep is awake.**

Word partners

sleep soundly/well
to sleep deeply and comfortably
If I have a lot of exercise, I sleep more soundly.

light sleeper
someone whose sleep is easily disturbed
Mum's a light sleeper.

nap
a short sleep, usually in the afternoon
Grandma likes to take a nap after lunch.

slumber (formal)
sleep
The princess ate the apple and fell into a deep slumber.

snooze
a short, light sleep
Dad had a snooze while we went out for a walk.

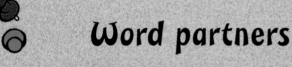

n o p q r **s** t u v w x y z

Small

dainty · little · meagre · miniature · minuscule · minute
puny · shrink · shrivel · tiny

dainty
small and delicate
The doll has dainty hands and long red hair.

little
not big
They live in a sweet little cottage.

meagre
not enough, too little
The farmers try to survive on their meagre harvest.

miniature
much smaller than normal
There is a miniature town in Denmark.

minuscule
very small
A baby panda is minuscule compared to its mother.

minute
very small and difficult to see
A cat's whiskers are covered in minute sensors.

puny
small and weak
Pat Rafter was called puny when he was a boy.

tiny
very small
Coral reefs are made up of thousands of tiny animals.

puny

In other words

small world

something you say when you meet someone who knows a person or a place you know and you are surprised
I don't believe you've met Sally too – what a small world!

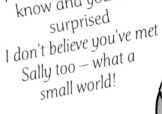

to become smaller

shrink

shrink
to get smaller because of the effects of water or heat
My T-shirt shrank in the wash – it's too small now.

shrivel
to get smaller and drier
Tomatoes shrivel up in very hot sun.

> **The opposite of small is large.**

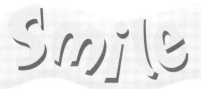

● **to smile because you are happy**

beam
to smile a big smile for a long time, usually because you are proud of something or someone
The parents beamed as their children went up to receive their prizes.

to break into a smile
to suddenly start smiling
She broke into a smile when she heard the good news.

Did you know?

In Old English 'smirk' was the word for 'smile', but not in the unpleasant way that we understand it now.

face lights up
to look happy suddenly
Their faces lit up as soon as they saw the lights on the tree.

grin
to smile a wide, happy smile
They grinned and waved when they saw us.

● **to smile in an unpleasant way**

simper
to smile in a foolish, annoying way
He simpered at the teacher.

The opposite of smile is frown.

smirk
to smile in a nasty way because you are pleased about someone else's bad luck
What are you smirking about?

sneer
to smile in an unpleasant way that shows that you don't respect someone or something
The giant sneered at the children as he passed.

In other words
to grin like a Cheshire cat
to smile very widely because you're pleased about something
This idiom comes from a character in Lewis Carroll's book *Alice's Adventures in Wonderland*. Alice goes to a land where nothing is normal and she meets a lot of strange characters. The Cheshire cat is one of these. He fades away as Alice is talking to him. The only thing left is his grin, floating in the air.

activate
to start something happening or working
The machine is activated by pressing this button.

begin
to start doing something
Begin the letter with 'Dear'.

commence
to start or begin (formal)
The ceremony will now commence.

embark on
to start a big, important job or a journey
Our school is embarking on a big recycling project.

initiate
to start something such as a discussion about something (formal)
A neighbouring country initiated the peace talks.

The opposites of start are finish and end.

launch

launch
to start something publicly
The ship was launched by the mayoress.

open
to begin to be shown, such as a film or a play
We want to see the film as soon as it opens.

set in motion
to start something like a process that will take a long time
The plan has been set in motion.

to start something in an organization

establish
to start something permanent
Oxford University was established more than 800 years ago.

found
to start something like a company or city
The company was founded in 1995.

set up
to make all the plans to start something
We've set up everything.

In other words

to give someone a head start (idiom)
to give someone an advantage
The hare was so confident of winning the race, he gave the tortoise a head start.

burglar · burgle · kleptomaniac · loot · mug · mugger
poach · rob · robber · shoplift · shoplifter · thief

● to steal

burgle
to steal things
from a place
such as a
house or office
*Our house was
burgled last night.*

burgle

loot
to steal things from
shops when the police are busy
because something else is happening
Shops were looted during the riots.

mug
to attack and steal from someone in the street
The man was mugged on his way to work.

In other words
tea leaf
Cockney rhyming slang for 'thief'.

daylight robbery (idiom)
very expensive
These prices are daylight robbery.

poach
to catch animals without permission
Poaching is a big problem in Africa.

rob
to steal something from a person or place
Police caught the gang that robbed the bank

shoplift
to steal things from a shop by hiding them
A boy was caught shoplifting.

● people who steal

burglar
a person who steals things from a building
The burglar got in through a window in the back.

kleptomaniac
a person who can't stop themselves stealing
Kleptomaniacs need professional help.

mugger
a person who steals money from people by
attacking them in the street
The mugger was put in jail.

robber
a person who steals things from a public place
The robbers wore masks.

shoplifter
a person who steals when they are in shops
The CCTVs are there to stop shoplifters.

thief
a general word for a person who steals things
Car thieves can steal a car very quickly.

Did you know?
The word 'steal' probably
comes from the Old English
stelan, and was was in use
before the 12th century.

stop

abandon · cease · drop · end · finish · halt · pause · quit · retire · stall

abandon
to stop doing something before it is finished because it is difficult
The team abandoned the search until the morning.

cease
to stop happening (formal)
Fighting has ceased.

drop
to stop doing something because it does not seem like a good thing to do
We've decided to drop plans for a concert until after the holidays.

end
to finish or stop
How does the story end?

finish
to stop doing something because it is complete
When you finish the test, turn the paper over.

halt
to stop moving
The procession halted.

halt

In other words

to stop someone in their tracks (idiom)
to surprise someone so suddenly that they stop what they are doing
A loud noise stopped us in our tracks.

pause
to stop temporarily
Pause, take a breath and then sing the next part.

quit
to stop doing something
Quit running, walk!

retire
to stop working
Grandma retired when she was sixty.

stall
to stop, usually an engine in a car or plane, because there is not enough power
Our car sometimes stalls on hills.

The opposites of stop are start and begin.

 **story**

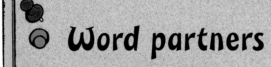 *anecdote · epic · fable · legend · myth · novel · saga · tale · yarn*

anecdote
a short, usually funny, story
He told an anecdote about his first day at school.

epic
a very long story about past times told in a poem, book or film
'Beowulf' is an epic poem that was written more than 1000 years ago.

fable
a story with a moral message, usually with animal characters instead of people
'Aesop's Fables' were not written down at first.

legend
a very old magical story
'William Tell' is a legend about a man who had to shoot an apple off his son's head.

myth
an ancient story
There are famous myths from ancient Greece, Rome and Scandinavia.

Word partners

a tall story
a story that is hard to believe because it is very exciting or unlikely
He tells such tall stories, it is difficult to believe a word he says.

novel
a book that is about imaginary people and things
Have you ever read a whole novel?

novel

saga
a story about a long period of time
A saga is often written about one family.

tale
an exciting story
My uncle tells tales about his adventures in Africa.

yarn
a long story about exciting things that are hard to believe
'Spinning yarns' means telling people stories that aren't true.

In other words

to cut a long story short (idiom)
to tell the main facts of a story leaving out most of the details
Anyway, to cut a long story short, we decided to come home early.

Stupid

words for describing ideas or other things that are not sensible

absurd
completely stupid
The plan is absolutely absurd – it'll never work.

daft
childishly stupid but sometimes funny (informal)
Michael is very bright but sometimes he has daft ideas.

daft

The opposites of stupid are sensible and intelligent.

foolish
stupid in a way that could cause problems in the future
I think it would be foolish to plant the seeds this early.

idiotic
very stupid, sometimes risky
He's always taking idiotic chances – he's a real daredevil.

ridiculous
unbelievably stupid
Don't be ridiculous – we can't be in two places at the same time.

silly
childishly stupid, sometimes in a funny way
We played a few silly games but they were fun.

unwise
stupid in a way that could cause problems (formal)
It is unwise to swim right after eating a big meal.

not intelligent

dim
slow to understand or learn (informal)
Now I understand, sorry to be so dim!

thick
not intelligent at all
He's not thick, just a little confused.

In other words

to play the fool (idiom)
to act in a silly way to make people laugh
Sam is always playing the fool.

surprised

amazed
so surprised you can't quite believe what's happened
We were amazed by some of his card tricks.

astonished
very surprised that something has happened
I'm astonished – I didn't expect to win.

amazed

astounded
very surprised
The listeners were astounded by the news.

shocked
very surprised by something bad
We were shocked by their behaviour.

speechless
so surprised that you can't talk
When they told us the price we were speechless.

taken aback
so surprised that you don't know what to say
I was a bit taken aback.

speechless

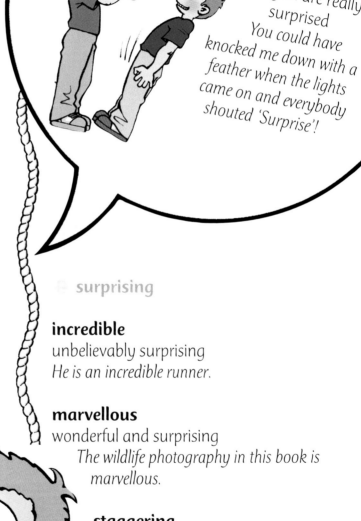

In other words

you could have knocked me down with a feather! (idiom)
something you say when you are really surprised
You could have knocked me down with a feather when the lights came on and everybody shouted 'Surprise'!

surprising

incredible
unbelievably surprising
He is an incredible runner.

marvellous
wonderful and surprising
The wildlife photography in this book is marvellous.

staggering
extremely surprising in a good or bad way
They spent a staggering amount of money.

stunning
very surprising
The special effects are stunning.

Take

carry · convey · deliver · fetch · guide · lead · shepherd · transport

carry

to take something from one place to another
The helicopter carried fresh supplies to the camp.

convey

to take something like liquid, electricity or gas from one place to another (formal)
The blood is conveyed from the heart through the arteries.

deliver

to take letters, parcels, newspapers and other things to a place
We delivered the Christmas cards on foot.

fetch

to go and get something and take it back to where you started
Our dog could fetch sticks all day long.

transport

to take lots of people or things from one place to another
Oil is transported in tankers.

Word partners

to take over
1. to be bossy
2. to take control of something
1. My sister keeps trying to take over.
2. Can you take over the driving in 10 minutes?

● **to take someone somewhere**

guide

to take someone to a place you know well
One of the Scouts guided us around the exhibition.

lead

to take someone somewhere by going in front of them
They led us out of the cave.

shepherd

to take a group of people somewhere
The teachers shepherded us towards the coach.

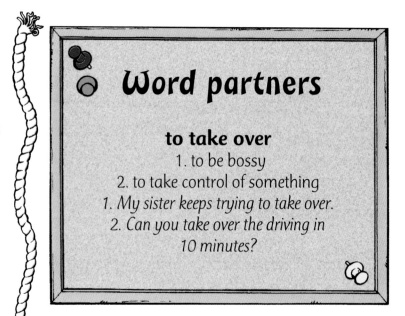

In other words

you can take a horse to water but you can't make him drink (saying)
you can give someone the chance to do something but you can't make them take it.

The opposite of take is give.

Talk

blab
to talk about something that you are not supposed to mention
Who blabbed?

chat
to talk in a friendly way
We were just chatting about the summer holidays.

converse
to talk to someone (formal)
Parents' day is a time when teachers and parents meet and converse.

Did you know?

'Talk' dates back to the 12th century. It is probably related to the Middle English word *tale*, which means 'story'.

gossip
to talk about other people's lives
I could tell they were gossiping about something when we walked in.

gossip

natter
to talk about things for fun (informal)
We sat and nattered all day.

In other words

can talk the hind legs off a donkey (idiom)
able to talk a lot
My Aunt Jo can talk the hind legs off a donkey.

rabbit
to keep talking about something, usually boring (informal)
What are you rabbiting on about now?

waffle
to talk about something without saying anything useful
He waffled on about badges.

witter
to talk for a long time without saying much
Jamie wittered on for hours.

Word partners

small talk
to make polite conversation about nothing in particular
The taxi driver made small talk as he drove us to the station.

t

Think

brood · consider · contemplate · meditate · ponder · reckon
reflect · regard · suspect · wonder

brood
to keep thinking about something that upsets you
Don't just sit there brooding – go and do something about it.

consider
to think about something that you might do
We're considering going to France this year.

brood

contemplate
to think seriously or deeply about something
They contemplated major changes.

meditate
to think deeply about something for a long time
A few minutes of meditation each day is really relaxing.

meditate

ponder
to think about a difficult question or a problem
He looked at the iron gate and pondered his escape.

reckon
to think that something is right or true
I reckon they'll get here in time.

reflect
to think carefully about something
We need time to reflect on what has happened.

regard
to have an opinion of someone or something
They don't think of it as work – they regard it as good fun.

suspect
to think that something is probably true
I suspect there will be a question about gravity in the test.

wonder
to try to guess what is happening or what will happen
I wonder where they've got to?

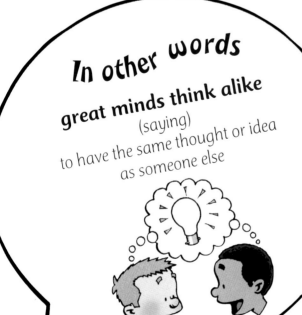

In other words

great minds think alike
(saying)
to have the same thought or idea as someone else

Throw

bowl · chuck · fling · heave · hurl · lob · pass
pelt · sling · toss

bowl
to throw a ball at a batman in cricket
Who's bowling for their team?

chuck
to throw something carelessly
Just chuck that stuff on the floor.

fling
to throw or move something forcefully
She flung her scarf around her neck.

chuck

heave
to throw something heavy
They heaved the sacks onto the back of the truck.

hurl
to throw something forcefully and violently
He hurled the spear at the target.

lob
to throw something high into the air
We lobbed the ball back over the fence.

pass
to throw the ball to another player on the same team
Quick, pass it over here!

pass

In other words

to throw in the towel (idiom)
to stop doing something because you don't think you can succeed
Tim got really tired and threw in the towel.

This comes from boxing. When a boxer's trainer throws a towel into the ring, it means the boxer is giving up.

pelt
to throw things at someone or something
The clowns pelted each other with tomatoes.

pelt

sling
to throw something carelessly
Don't just sling the book down on the table, put it on the bookshelf.

toss
to throw something with a quick, small movement
Toss me that cushion, will you?

t

Tired

beat · drained · drowsy · exhausted · flagging · shattered
sleepy · weary · tired out · worn out

beat
so tired that you want to stop what you're doing
(informal)
Sorry, I've got to rest, I'm beat.

drained
tired, without any energy
left
I felt drained after karate class.

drowsy
tired and sleepy
*The heat of the fire made us feel
drowsy so we went up to bed.*

exhausted
very tired after doing something
that used up your energy
*You walked all the way?
You must be exhausted.*

drained

In other words

to be sick and tired of something
(idiom)
to feel angry or bored because something
has been happening for a long time
*I'm sick and tired of
all this ironing.*

flagging
starting to lose energy
*During the tie-breaker, you
could see she was flagging.*

shattered
very tired (informal)
*I'm absolutely shattered, let's stay
at home.*

flagging

sleepy

sleepy

sleepy
ready to go to sleep
Go on up to bed, you look sleepy.

weary
tired after doing something for
a long time
*We'd been walking all day and
were weary and our feet hurt.*

tired/worn out
very tired after a lot of physical effort
That's it. We've got to stop – I'm tired out.

Travel

commute · crossing · excursion · explore · journey · outing
tour · trip · voyage · wander

● to travel

commute
to travel to and from work
Dad commutes to the city every day.

commute

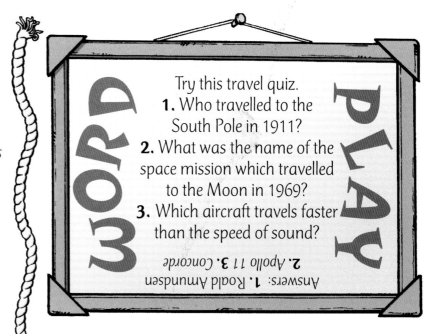

explore
to travel to find out more about a place
We'll have time to really explore the island.

wander
to travel round without a plan
Dad hired a car and we just wandered along the coast for a week.

outing
a short trip or visit to a place, usually nearby
There is a class outing on Friday to the castle.

tour
a visit to and around a place
We went on a tour of the city.

● types of travel

crossing
a trip in a boat or a ship across water from one side to the other
It was a rough crossing because of the storm.

excursion
short trip to visit a place
We have an excursion every term.

journey
travel from one place to another, usually far away
The journey was long but interesting.

trip
travel to a place, usually for a short time
Mum is on a business trip.

voyage
a long journey in a ship or spacecraft
Astronauts have to train for space voyages.

crossing

t

Understand

absorb
to learn and understand new information
There was a lot to absorb on the first day.

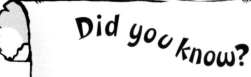

Did you know?

We can understand Egyptian hieroglyphs because of the Rosetta Stone, found in 1799. It is an ancient stone with the same message carved in three different writing systems.

appreciate
to understand someone's feelings or their situation
Teachers appreciate that a child's first day at school can be confusing.

comprehend
to understand something difficult or complicated (formal)
They were too young to comprehend what was happening.

digest
to think carefully about and understand new information
They'll need time to digest the report.

follow
to understand something (like a story) that has more than one point
Do you follow so far?

digest

get
to understand a story, joke or the reason for something
I didn't get the joke.

grasp
to clearly understand something difficult
They didn't grasp the full importance of the new law.

make sense of
to understand something because you have thought about it
I'm just beginning to make sense of how this computer game works.

realize
to understand something that you didn't before
I didn't realize we were supposed to complete all four questions.

see
to understand what something means or the reason for it
So you see, we need to keep a clear record of each student's project.

WORD PLAY

Can you understand this text message?

C U L8R.
R U OK?

Answer: See you later. Are you ok?

Value

advantage · benefit · cherish · esteem · merit · precious
priceless · prize · treasure · worth

● value

advantage
something that is valuable and will help you succeed
Playing the match at home is an advantage.

benefit
something that helps you
We have the benefit of good sports facilities.

esteem
respect and admiration
Dad's boss holds him in high esteem.

merit
valuable qualities of something or someone (formal)
The idea has merit.

worth
the value of something
The thieves took £1000 worth of mobile phones.

esteem

● to value

cherish
to value or love something very much
Mum cherishes the photos of us when we were little.

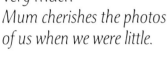

cherish

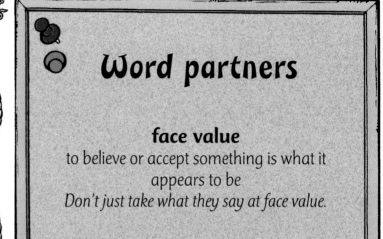

Word partners

face value
to believe or accept something is what it appears to be
Don't just take what they say at face value.

prize
to feel that something is important or valuable
Grandad prizes his rosebushes.

treasure
to feel that something is very valuable and gives you a lot of pleasure
We treasure the memories of the time we spent living in Africa.

● valuable

precious
extremely valuable, usually because it is something that is expensive or rare
Diamonds, emeralds and rubies are all kinds of precious stones.

priceless
so valuable that no price can be put on it
There are lots of priceless Roman artefacts in the museum.

Very

absolutely · completely · decidedly · highly · noticeably · particularly
quite · really · remarkably · terribly · truly

absolutely/completely
in every way
I completely forgot her birthday last year.

decidedly
very much, in an obvious way
He is playing decidedly better this season.

highly (formal or technical)
very
The programmers are highly skilled.

noticeably
very, in a way that is easy to see
The sports centre is noticeably busier in the school holidays.

particularly
especially
The judges were particularly impressed with her gymnastic routine.

> **The opposites of very are hardly and slightly.**

quite
very much
They are twins but their personalities are quite different.

really
very (informal)
It's really hot in here – can I open the window?

remarkably
very much so, in a surprising way
The results were remarkably good this year.

really

Did you know?
We don't use 'very' with words that already have a strong meaning. For example, we don't say *'I was very astounded.'* or *'We were very terrified.'* Instead we say something such as, *'I was completely astounded.'* or *'We were absolutely terrified.'*

terribly
very, usually used only in spoken English
I'm terribly sorry I was late – I overslept.

truly
very (formal)
I'm truly sorry.

truly

Wait

await · delay · hesitate · hold on · linger · pause · queue

await
to wait for something (formal)
The court is awaiting the jury's decision.

hold on
used to tell someone to wait for a short time (informal)
Hold on a minute, I'll just check for you.

queue
to stand in a line waiting for something
We had to queue for two hours.

to wait or make someone wait before doing something

delay
to cause something to be late
We were delayed by traffic.

delay

hesitate
to wait a little before doing something, usually because you are not sure
Lily hesitated before choosing a library book.

linger
to wait for extra time before leaving a place
Fans lingered, hoping to get an autograph.

In other words

he who hesitates is lost
(saying)
If you don't do something when you get the chance, you might not get the chance again.

pause
to wait for a while before continuing to do something
The lion paused and looked around.

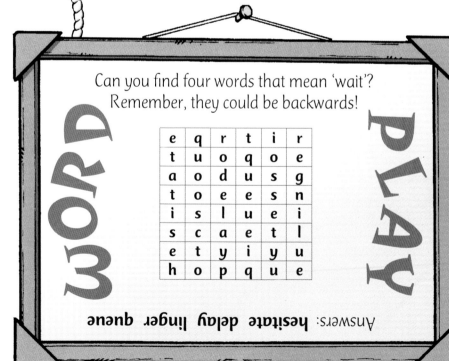

WORD PLAY

Can you find four words that mean 'wait'?
Remember, they could be backwards!

e	q	r	t	i	r
t	u	o	q	o	e
a	o	d	u	s	g
t	o	e	e	s	n
i	s	l	u	e	i
s	c	a	e	t	l
e	t	y	i	y	u
h	o	p	q	u	e

Answers: **hesitate delay linger queue**

Walk

creep · hike · limp · march · stride · stroll · tiptoe · trek · wade · wander

creep
to walk quietly, slowly and secretly
We crept up and jumped in front of them.

creep

hike
to walk a long way, usually in the country
We hiked up the hill and found a good place for our picnic.

limp
to walk dragging one foot because it hurts
David limped off the pitch.

march
to walk together using strong, regular steps
The soldiers marched past the flag.

stride
to walk confidently with big steps
He strode into the room.

stroll
to walk slowly and comfortably
We strolled through the park.

tiptoe
to walk on your toes, trying not to make a noise
I took off my shoes and tiptoed past their room.

tiptoe

In other words

walk the plank (idiom)
to be forced to do something
This comes from the great age of sailing ships, when someone who did something wrong would have to walk out on a long board (plank) and jump into the water.

trek
to walk a long way, especially in hills or mountains
I'd like to trek in the Himalayas.

wade
to walk through water
I had to wade into the pond to get the ball.

wander
to walk without a purpose or because you are lost
They wandered in the forest for hours before they found the camp.

aspire to · crave · desire · fancy · hanker after · impulse · long for
whim · wish for · yearn for

aspire to
to want or hope to do something or be something and work towards it
The story is about a girl who aspired to stardom.

crave
to want something so much that you can't think about anything else
I woke up craving chocolate.

crave

desire
to want something very much
You can find whatever you desire. There's something for everyone.

fancy
to want something (informal)
I fancy a walk, want to come?

hanker after
to think about something that you want but can't have
After a week at school, we were hankering after Mum's cooking.

hanker after

long for
to want something very much
We long for the summer holidays.

WORD PLAY

Unscramble the letters to find four words that mean 'want'.

1. ynera
2. sedrei
3. cevar
4. yfnca

Answers: 1. yearn 2. desire 3. crave 4. fancy

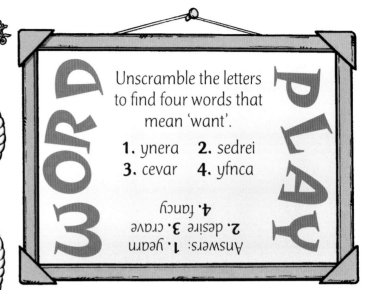

wish for
to want something to happen
I wish they'd hurry up and get here.

yearn for
to want something so much that you feel sad without it
The prisoners yearned for freedom.

yearn for

● a feeling of wanting something

impulse
a sudden feeling that you want to do or have something, without stopping to think whether it is a good idea
I bought it on impulse – now I don't like it.

whim
a sudden feeling that you want to do or have something
You can't just decide to get a puppy on a whim.

clammy · damp · drenched · humid · moist · muggy · saturated soaked · sodden · waterlogged

clammy
wet and sticky
When I'm nervous, the palms of my hands get clammy.

damp
slightly wet
These clothes are still damp from the rain.

clammy

drenched
extremely wet
The rain was so heavy we got absolutely drenched in no time.

In other words

wet behind the ears
(idiom)
young and inexperienced
It's his first day working here. He's a little wet behind the ears.

moist
slightly wet
Keep the soil moist.

saturated
completely wet
When the cloth is saturated, wring it out.

The opposite of wet is dry.

soaked
very wet
The cushions in the garden got soaked overnight.

sodden
wet and heavy
The bottom of the box is sodden.

Word partners

a wet blanket
someone who stops other people from having fun
Look, I don't mean to be a wet blanket but turn the music down.

waterlogged
so wet that something cannot hold more water
The pitch is waterlogged, so the match is postponed.

wet weather

humid
wet and hot
The coast is hot and humid at this time of year.

muggy
unpleasantly wet and warm
We don't like playing when it's hot and muggy.

win

achievement · conquest · landslide · success · sweep the board
triumph · victory · walkover · win easily

a win

achievement
something that you succeed in doing
Setting a new school record was quite an achievement.

conquest
a victory, usually when a country takes control of a place after winning a battle
The Norman Conquest was led by William the Conqueror.

landslide
when one side or candidate gets many more votes than another
Yes! We won by a landslide!

success
a win, especially in a series of games, matches or fights
It was our third match and our third success.

victory
a win, especially in a competition or battle
The streets were full of people celebrating the victory.

walkover
a very easy win, especially in sport
The set was a walkover for her.

walkover

In other words

to win something hands down (idiom)
to win easily
Imogen won the race hands down!

The opposite of win is lose.

to win

win easily
to win a race or game without a lot of difficulty
They won the first few events easily.

sweep the board
to win all the points, medals or prizes
James swept the board on sports day.

triumph
to win something difficult or important
It was a great triumph for their team.

Work

to be industrious
to work hard and get things done
It looks great in here — you've been very industrious.

labour
to work hard, usually doing something physical
The farmers labour long hours during harvest.

push yourself
to force yourself to work hard
I was tired and really had to push myself to finish.

push yourself

slave away
to work extremely hard at something that you do not enjoy (informal)
The sailors slaved away at the oars.

toil
to do boring work for a long time (formal)
In Colonial times, thousands of people toiled in the plantations.

a task

drudgery
work that is physically hard and boring
Working in Victorian factories was drudgery for many people.

duties
things that you have to do as part of your job
Everyone in the class has different duties.

grind
boring work
Memorising your times tables is a grind but it pays off.

grind

In other words

beaver away at (idiom)
to work very hard at something
He beavered away at his homework for hours.

This comes from the way beavers work when they build complicated dams.

Young

● **a young person**

adolescent
a young person who is developing into an adult
Teenagers are adolescents.

infant
a baby or young child
I don't remember living there because I was an infant when we left.

juvenile
a young person
There are special rules for juveniles.

kid
a child (informal)
Don't be too hard on him — he's just a kid.

minor
a legal term for a person who is not an adult
Minors must be accompanied by an adult.

infant

WORD PLAY

Unscramble the letters to find four names of young animals.

1. legipt 2. loaf
3. eldpoat 4. lcfa

Answers: 1. piglet 2. foal
3. tadpole 4. calf

The opposite of
young is old.

● **young**

little
a sister or brother who is younger than you.
My little brother is learning to walk.

small
young, usually less than 10 years old
Dad says that when he was small, he couldn't swim.

small

Word partners

young at heart
to feel very young, even if you are not
I may be getting older, but I'm young at heart.

Index

All the headwords and branchwords (synonyms) in your book are listed here alphabetically. Simply look up the word you want to use – the headword for that entry is listed opposite in **bold** type.

cross-section see **Part**
crowd see **Friend**
crucial see **Important**
crumb see **Part**
cry see **Call**
cunning see **Clever**
currency see **Money**

Dd

daft see **Stupid**
dainty see **Small**
damp see **Wet**
dash see **Fast**
dash see **Run**
daydream see **Imagine**
deafening see **Loud**
decent see **Good**
decidedly see **Very**
dejected see **Sad**
delay see **Wait**
delighted see **Happy**
deliver see **Promise**
deliver see **Take**
demanding see **Difficult**
demolish see **Eat**
deposit see **Payment**
deposit see **Put**
depressed see **Sad**
deprived see **Poor**
desire see **Want**
desolate see **Sad**
despise see **Hate**
despondent see **Sad**
destitute see **Poor**
detest see **Hate**
devour see **Eat**
different see **Different**
difficult see **Difficult**
digest see **Understand**
dim see **Stupid**
disadvantaged see **Poor**
dispute see **Argue**
dissimilar see **Different**
distinctive see **Different**
distribute see **Give**
diverse see **Different**
a doddle see **Easy**
donate see **Give**
doting see **Love**
down see **Sad**
doze see **Sleep**
drain see **Drink**
drained see **Tired**
draughty see **Cold**
dreadful see **Bad**
dreading see **Frightened**
dream of see **Imagine**
drenched see **Wet**
drift off see **Sleep**
drink see **Drink**
drop see **Stop**
drop off see **Sleep**
drowsy see **Sleep**

drudgery see **Work**
duties see **Work**
duty see **Job**

Ee

ear-splitting see **Loud**
easy see **Easy**
eat see **Eat**
ecstatic see **Happy**
effortless see **Easy**
elderly see **Old**
element see **Part**
embark on see **Start**
end see **Stop**
enquire see **Ask**
epic see **Story**
equivalent see **Same**
errand see **Job**
error see **Mistake**
establish see **Start**
esteem see **Value**
everyday see **Ordinary**
examine see **Look**
excellent see **Good**
exclaim see **Say**
excursion see **Travel**
exhausted see **Tired**
expert see **Know**
explore see **Travel**

Ff

fable see **Story**
face lights up see **Smile**
family see **Person**
fancy see **Want**
fantasize see **Imagine**
fantastic see **Good**
fashion see **Make**
fast see **Fast**
fault see **Mistake**
fed up see **Sad**
fee see **Payment**
feed see **Eat**
feel see **Know**
fetch see **Carry**
fetch see **Take**
feud see **Argue**
fiddly see **Difficult**
fight see **Argue**
figure see **Money**
fine see **Payment**
finish see **Stop**
fitting see **Right**
flagging see **Tired**
flee see **Run**
fling see **Throw**
flush see **Rich**
folks see **Person**
follow see **Understand**
foolish see **Stupid**
force see **Open**
form see **Make**
fortune see **Money**

found see **Start**
fraction see **Part**
freezing see **Cold**
fresh see **New**
friend see **Friend**
frightened see **Frightened**
frosty see **Cold**
fun see **Good**
funny see **Funny**
furious see **Angry**
furtive see **Secret**

Gg

gaffe see **Mistake**
gag see **Joke**
gallop see **Run**
gang see **Friend**
gaze see **look**
generate see **Make**
genuine see **Real**
geriatric see **Old**
get see **Understand**
ghastly see **Bad**
giggle see **Laugh**
give see **Give**
give your word see **Promise**
glad see **Happy**
glance see **Look**
glare see **Look**
glimpse see **Look**
glum see **Sad**
go through with see **Promise**
gobble see **Eat**
good see **Good**
goof see **Mistake**
goosepimples see **Cold**
gossip see **Talk**
grasp see **Understand**
great see **Good**
grin see **Smile**
grind see **Work**
gruelling see **Difficult**
guarantee see **Promise**
guffaw see **Laugh**
guide see **Take**
gulp see **Drink**
guzzle see **Drink**

Hh

hair-raising see **Frightened**
hallucinate see **Imagine**
halt see **Stop**
hand see **Give**
handy see **Near**
hanker after see **Want**
happy see **Happy**
hard see **Difficult**
hate see **Hate**
haughty see **Proud**
haul see **Carry**
haunting see **Remember**
heap see **Put**
heartfelt see **Real**

heave   see **Throw**
hero/heroine   see **Person**
hesitate   see **Wait**
hibernate   see **Sleep**
hidden   see **Secret**
high speed   see **Fast**
highly   see **Very**
hike   see **Walk**
hilarious   see **Funny**
hint   see **Say**
historic   see **Old**
hold on   see **Wait**
homesick   see **Sad**
hop   see **Jump**
hopeless   see **Bad**
hospitable   see **Friend**
hot   see **Hot**
human   see **Person**
humanity   see **Person**
humankind   see **Person**
humid   see **Hot**
humorous   see **Funny**
hurdle   see **Jump**
hurl   see **Throw**
hushed   see **Quiet**
hush-hush   see **Secret**

Ii

identical   see **Same**
identity   see **Name**
idiotic   see **Stupid**
idiot-proof   see **Easy**
imagine   see **Imagine**
important   see **Important**
impossible   see **Difficult**
impoverished   see **Poor**
impressive   see **Good**
impulse   see **Want**
in jest   see **Joke**
in private   see **Secret**
in the vicinity   see **Near**
inaudible   see **Quiet**
incredible   see **Good**
incredible   see **Surprised**
indignant   see **Angry**
individual   see **Different**
individual   see **Person**
industrious   see **Work**
inept   see **Bad**
inferior   see **Bad**
ingredient   see **Part**
initial   see **Name**
initiate   see **Start**
innovative   see **New**
inspect   see **Look**
instalments   see **Payment**
intellectual   see **Clever**
intelligent   see **Clever**
interrogate   see **Ask**
interview   see **Ask**
irate   see **Angry**
irritated   see **Angry**

Jj

job   see **Job**
jog   see **Run**
joke   see **Joke**
joking   see **Joke**
jolly   see **Happy**
journey   see **Travel**
jump   see **Jump**
just   see **Right**
just out   see **New**

Kk

key   see **Important**
kip   see **Sleep**
kidding   see **Joke**
kleptomaniac   see **Steal**
know   see **Know**
knowledgeable   see **Clever**

Ll

labour   see **Work**
landslide   see **Win**
lap up   see **Drink**
latest   see **New**
laugh   see **Laugh**
launch   see **Start**
lay   see **Put**
lead   see **Take**
lean   see **Put**
leap   see **Jump**
legend   see **Story**
lift   see **Carry**
light-hearted   see **Funny**
limp   see **Walk**
linger   see **Wait**
little   see **Young**
livid   see **Angry**
loathe   see **Hate**
lob   see **Throw**
local   see **Near**
long for   see **Want**
look   see **Look**
loot   see **Money**
lope   see **Run**
loud   see **Loud**
love   see **Love**
lovely   see **Good**
low   see **Quiet**
low   see **Sad**
lug   see **Carry**
lukewarm   see **Hot**

Mm

mad   see **Angry**
maiden name   see **Name**
major   see **Important**
make   see **Make**
make sense of   see **Understand**
a man of means   see **Rich**
manufacture   see **Make**
march   see **Walk**
marvellous   see **Good**
marvellous   see **Surprised**

mate   see **Friend**
meagre   see **Small**
meditate   see **Think**
memorable   see **Remember**
mention   see **Say**
merit   see **Value**
miniature   see **Small**
minuscule   see **Small**
minute   see **Small**
miserable   see **Sad**
misjudge   see **Mistake**
mission   see **Job**
mistake   see **Mistake**
mix-up   see **Mistake**
moist   see **Wet**
money   see **Money**
mould   see **Make**
move   see **Move**
muffled   see **Quiet**
mug   see **Steal**
mugger   see **Steal**
muggy   see **Wet**
mumble   see **Say**
munch   see **Eat**
mundane   see **Ordinary**
muted   see **Quiet**
mutter   see **Say**
myth   see **Story**

Nn

name   see **Call**
name   see **Name**
namesake   see **Name**
nap   see **Sleep**
natter   see **Talk**
naughty   see **Bad**
near   see **Near**
nearby   see **Near**
needy   see **Poor**
neighbouring   see **Near**
neighbourly   see **Friend**
neutral   see **Ordinary**
new   see **New**
newcomer   see **New**
next   see **Near**
nibble   see **Eat**
nice   see **Good**
nickname   see **Name**
noisy   see **loud**
normal   see **Ordinary**
not at all like   see **Different**
notable   see **Important**
noticeably   see **Very**
novel   see **New**
novel   see **Story**
occupation   see **Job**

Oo

old   see **Old**
open   see **Open**
open   see **Start**
ordinary   see **Ordinary**
original   see **New**

outing — see **Travel**
outstanding — see **Good**
overjoyed — see **Happy**
oversight — see **Mistake**

Pp

painless — see **Easy**
pal — see **Friend**
panic-stricken — see **Frightened**
part — see **Part**
particularly — see **Very**
pass — see **Throw**
pass on — see **Give**
pause — see **Stop**
pause — see **Wait**
payment — see **Payment**
peek — see **Look**
peep — see **Look**
peer — see **Look**
pelt — see **Throw**
pen name — see **Name**
penetrating — see **Loud**
penniless — see **Poor**
person — see **Person**
petrified — see **Loud**
phone — see **Call**
pick a lock — see **Open**
picture — see **Imagine**
piercing — see **Loud**
pile — see **Put**
pioneering — see **New**
place — see **Put**
plead — see **Ask**
pleased — see **Happy**
pledge — see **Promise**
poach — see **Steal**
pocket money — see **Money**
polish off — see **Drink**
poll — see **Ask**
pompous — see **Proud**
ponder — see **Think**
poor — see **Poor**
portion — see **Part**
position — see **Put**
pounce — see **Jump**
practical joke — see **Joke**
prank — see **Joke**
precious — see **Value**
present — see **Give**
priceless — see **Value**
prise — see **Open**
prize — see **Value**
produce — see **Make**
profession — see **Job**
project — see **Job**
promise — see **Promise**
prompt — see **Remember**
prop — see **Put**
proper — see **Right**
prosperous — see **Rich**
proud — see **Proud**
pseudonym — see **Name**
pump — see **Ask**

pun — see **Joke**
punch line — see **Joke**
puny — see **Small**
push yourself — see **Work**
put — see **Put**

Qq

quarrel — see **Argue**
quench — see **Drink**
query — see **Ask**
question — see **Ask**
queue — see **Wait**
quick — see **Clever**
quick — see **Fast**
quickly — see **Fast**
quiet — see **Quiet**
quit — see **Stop**
quite — see **Very**
quiz — see **Ask**

Rr

rabbit — see **Talk**
race — see **Run**
rapid — see **Fast**
real — see **Real**
realize — see **Know**
realize — see **Understand**
really — see **Very**
recall — see **Remember**
recent — see **New**
reckon — see **Think**
recollect — see **Remember**
reflect — see **Think**
refund — see **Payment**
regard — see **Think**
relive — see **Remember**
relocate — see **Move**
remark — see **Say**
remarkably — see **Very**
remember — see **Remember**
remind — see **Remember**
reminisce — see **Remember**
resentful — see **Angry**
retire — see **Stop**
reward — see **Give**
rich — see **Rich**
riddle — see **Joke**
ridiculous — see **Stupid**
right — see **Right**
ring — see **Call**
roar with laughter — see **Laugh**
roasting — see **Hot**
rob — see **Steal**
robber — see **Steal**
routine — see **Ordinary**
row — see **Argue**
rowdy — see **Loud**
run — see **Run**
rush — see **Fast**
rush — see **Run**

Ss

sad — see **Sad**

saga — see **Story**
salary — see **Payment**
same — see **Same**
saturated — see **Wet**
say — see **Say**
scalding — see **Hot**
scared — see **Frightened**
scary — see **Frightened**
scoff — see **Eat**
scream — see **Call**
second-hand — see **Old**
secret — see **Secret**
section — see **Part**
see — see **Look**
see — see **Understand**
seething — see **Angry**
segment — see **Part**
sense — see **Know**
set in motion — see **Start**
set up — see **Start**
share out — see **Give**
shattered — see **Tired**
shepherd — see **Take**
shift — see **Move**
shivering — see **Cold**
shocked — see **Surprised**
shoplift — see **Steal**
shoplifter — see **Steal**
shout — see **Call**
shriek — see **Call**
shrink — see **Small**
shrivel — see **Small**
significant — see **Important**
silent — see **Quiet**
silly — see **Stupid**
simper — see **Smile**
simple — see **Easy**
sincere — see **Real**
sip — see **Drink**
skip — see **Jump**
sleep — see **Sleep**
sleepy — see **Sleep**
sling — see **Throw**
slip — see **Give**
slip — see **Mistake**
slumber — see **Sleep**
small — see **Small**
smarmy — see **Friend**
smart — see **Clever**
smile — see **Smile**
smirk — see **Smile**
smug — see **Proud**
snack — see **Eat**
sneer — see **Smile**
snigger — see **Laugh**
snobbish — see **Proud**
snooze — see **Sleep**
soaked — see **Wet**
sociable — see **Friend**
sodden — see **Wet**
soft — see **Quiet**
solid — see **Real**
somebody — see **Person**

spat	see **Argue**
specialist	see **Know**
speechless	see **Surprised**
speedy	see **Fast**
spicy	see **Hot**
spooky	see **Frightened**
spot	see **Look**
spring	see **Remember**
sprint	see **Run**
spy	see **Look**
squabble	see **Argue**
squirm	see **Move**
stack	see **Put**
staggering	see **Surprised**
stall	see **Stop**
stand	see **put**
stand by	see **Promise**
standard	see **Ordinary**
stare	see **Look**
start	see **Start**
steal	see **Steal**
still	see **Quiet**
stir	see **Move**
stop	see **Stop**
story	see **Story**
straightforward	see **Easy**
streetwise	see **Clever**
strenuous	see **Difficult**
stride	see **Walk**
stroll	see **Walk**
study	see **Look**
stunning	see **Surprised**
stupid	see **Stupid**
subdued	see **Quiet**
success	see **Win**
suitable	see **Right**
sum	see **Money**
summon	see **Call**
superior	see **Proud**
supersonic	see **Fast**
support	see **Carry**
surprised	see **Surprised**
surrounding	see **Remember**
survey	see **Ask**
suspect	see **Think**
swallow	see **Drink**
swear	see **Promise**
sweep the board	see **Win**
sweltering	see **Hot**
swig	see **Drink**
swing	see **Move**
synonym	see **Same**

Tt

taciturn	see **Quiet**
take	see **Carry**
take	see **Take**
taken aback	see **Surprised**
tale	see **Story**
talented	see **Good**
talk	see **Talk**
task	see **Job**
tear	see **Run**

tell	see **Say**
tender	see **Love**
terrible	see **Bad**
terribly	see **Very**
terrified	see **Frightened**
thick	see **Stupid**
thief	see **Steal**
think	see **Think**
thrilled	see **Happy**
throw	see **Throw**
thunderous	see **Loud**
tiff	see **Argue**
tiny	see **Small**
tip	see **Payment**
tiptoe	see **Walk**
tired	see **Tired**
tired out	see **Tired**
titter	see **Laugh**
toil	see **Work**
too big for your boots	see **Proud**
toss	see **Throw**
tote	see **Carry**
tough	see **Difficult**
tour	see **Travel**
trade	see **Job**
transfer	see **Move**
transport	see **Carry**
transport	see **Move**
transport	see **Take**
travel	see **Travel**
treasure	see **Value**
trek	see **Walk**
tricky	see **Difficult**
trip	see **Travel**
triumph	see **Win**
true	see **Real**
truly	see **Very**

Uu

unbolt	see **Open**
uncomplicated	see **Easy**
underprivileged	see **Poor**
understand	see **Understand**
undertake	see **Promise**
undertaking	see **Job**
unfold	see **Open**
unforgettable	see **Remember**
unhappy	see **Sad**
unique	see **Different**
unlock	see **Open**
unscrew	see **Open**
unwise	see **Stupid**
unwrap	see **Open**
used	see **Old**
useless	see **Bad**
user-friendly	see **Easy**

Vv

vain	see **Proud**
value	see **Value**
vary	see **Different**
vault	see **Jump**

verbatim	see **Same**
very	see **Very**
veteran	see **Old**
victory	see **Win**
vintage	see **Old**
visualize	see **Imagine**
vital	see **Important**
vocation	see **Job**
vow	see **Promise**
voyage	see **Travel**

Ww

wade	see **Walk**
waffle	see **Talk**
wages	see **Payment**
wait	see **Wait**
walk	see **Walk**
walkover	see **Win**
wander	see **Travel**
wander	see **Walk**
want	see **Want**
warm	see **Hot**
waterlogged	see **Wet**
wealth	see **Money**
wealthy	see **Rich**
weary	see **Tired**
weighty	see **Important**
well-heeled	see **Rich**
well-off	see **Rich**
wet	see **Wet**
whim	see **Want**
whisper	see **Say**
wide open	see **Open**
win	see **Win**
wisecrack	see **Joke**
wish for	see **Want**
within walking distance	see **Near**
witter	see **Talk**
witty	see **Funny**
wonder	see **Think**
wonderful	see **Good**
word for word	see **Same**
work	see **Work**
worn out	see **Tired**
worship	see **Love**
worth	see **Value**
wriggle	see **Move**
writhe	see **Move**

Yy

yarn	see **Story**
yearn for	see **Want**
yell	see **Call**